SECRETS OF GREAT SALESPEOPLE

50 Ways to Sell Business-to-Business

Jeremy Raymond has been a deputy headteacher, a management consultant, a managing director, an executive coach and an author – and each of these jobs involved selling. When he worked at PWC he realized that, if he wanted an interesting and varied career, he had better master the art of developing business.
From selling himself he progressed to selling ideas, projects and solutions to clients like IBM, Ford and Novartis. He has even sold training programmes to pass on these skills to other professionals. He believes selling should be enjoyable for both salespeople and their clients, and that identifying solutions that help your client's business to grow is a worthwhile professional job.

Acknowledgements and admissions

Most useful wisdom on a subject is the work of many, on whose shoulders you have stood. I have learned about selling from my own experience, but also from colleagues, clients, teachers and other authors and I have borrowed copiously from my observations of them at work, their comments and suggestions.
The list is long but I would particularly like to mention those who have, knowingly or not, contributed to this book: Bill Allan, Stephen Bishop, Ian Bradley, Roger Cooke, Sheldon Franklin, Mike Griffiths, Janice Hughes, William Johnson, Kip Meek, David Matthews, James Peverell, Lawrie Phillpott, Joanne Russell, John Rushton, Josh Smith, Mike Shank, Atif Sheikh, Crispin Tweddell, Garnet Twigg, Andrew Tyler, Josh Smith, Harith Viswarnath and Midge Wilker, who showed me that selling can be fun.

I have represented most contributions anonymously, as interviewees generally requested, but also because I have used my own words to express others' useful ideas and stories. These words are often assumptive and, as storytelling is part of selling, I hope this is fair play. If there is wisdom here, it is theirs. If there is froth, it is mine.

Finally, I would like to thank Linda for putting up with me during the struggle that is any book's creation. In sales terms, a book is a one-sided deal, but I dedicate it to her with my love and gratitude.

SECRETS OF GREAT SALESPEOPLE

50 Ways to Sell Business-to-Business

Jeremy Raymond

First published in Great Britain in 2016 by John Murray Learning. An Hachette UK company.

British Library Cataloguing in Publication Data: a catalogue record for this title is available from the British Library.

Library of Congress Catalog Card Number: on file.

Paperback ISBN: 978 1 473 61163 4

eBook ISBN: 978 1 473 61164 1

3

The publisher has used its best endeavours to ensure that any website addresses referred to in this book are correct and active at the time of going to press. However, the publisher and the author have no responsibility for the websites and can make no guarantee that a site will remain live or that the content will remain relevant, decent or appropriate.

The publisher has made every effort to mark as such all words which it believes to be trademarks. The publisher should also like to make it clear that the presence of a word in the book, whether marked or unmarked, in no way affects its legal status as a trademark.

Every reasonable effort has been made by the publisher to trace the copyright holders of material in this book. Any errors or omissions should be notified in writing to the publisher, who will endeavour to rectify the situation for any reprints and future editions.

Typeset by Cenveo® Publisher Services.

Printed and bound in Great Britain by CPI Group (UK) Ltd., Croydon CR0 4YY.

John Murray Learning policy is to use papers that are natural, renewable and recyclable products and made from wood grown in sustainable forests. The logging and manufacturing processes are expected to conform to the environmental regulations of the country of origin.

John Murray Learning
Carmelite House
50 Victoria Embankment
London
EC4Y 0DZ
www.hodder.co.uk

Also available
in ebook

CONTENTS

INTRODUCTION

Trade brings people together. It builds relationships between individuals, communities, organizations and nations. Nomadic people bartered with their surplus for what they didn't have, even if that surplus was sometimes daughters. Later, there was trade within communities – shops and markets – and trade between communities – travelling salespeople, merchant adventurers. Vasco da Gama, Magellan, Christopher Columbus and many before them, were not just sailors: they were salesmen. Over time people build trust with the exchange of goods or services and recommend these people to others, and both parties benefit, while the world becomes more closely and peacefully knit. We are a social species. Exchanges build ties. Trade is in our nature.

The Industrial Revolution changed things. Before then, when every table was made to order by a carpenter, as a customer you had to have a relationship with the producer, who was also the salesperson. Treat your producer badly and your table might have a wobble. When goods are mass-produced, they are no longer linked to individual demand. Selling is divorced from buying; it aims to move goods off the salesperson's balance sheet and on to that of the customer. Salespeople are not part of the buyer's community; there are no personal consequences for them in 'shifting tin', as the old IBM salespeople used to call it. The sales 'rep' is interested only in his own short-term gain, managed by commission. Trade becomes less about harmony and long-term accord, let alone matrimony and romance; it is a one-night stand, a contest, with losers as well as winners.

The popular stereotype of salespeople is the legacy of this revolution in production. Wily, mistrusted, they roam the desolate forecourts of imagined second-hand car dealerships. If your job is to sell, you may often feel misunderstood. However, you are critical to the wealth of companies and nations. Where would those sneering types be without your ability to provide secure work for them? Without your efforts, companies would not succeed and grow, shareholder returns would fall, pensioners would go hungry... (Salespeople have always been prone to a little exaggeration.)

Today we are in the throes of a digital revolution. The high-street shops slowly disappear under the influence of online buying. Sites like Amazon are so simple, so easy to use. The values of convenience supplant the more human benefits of trade. Click and collect. Click and send. Customers purchase products, often just as tailored to their specifications as the handmade tables of old, and all without delay, without face-to-face discussion, without feeling. Surf the Net. Lowest price wins.

Of course, the changes to trading, buying and selling aren't as simple as this three-stage transition makes out. *All* previous forms of trade continue to coexist. Your great-grandmother shopped in the weekly market, your grandmother probably went to a local grocery store, your mother shopped in the supermarket and you buy online. There are still Marco Polos out there finding new markets; they are more likely to be app developers than merchant adventurers, but the expansion of trade is unstoppable.

Business-to-business (B2B) trade – the subject of this book – has gone through similar revolutions. On the selling side, new jobs emerged as deals grew larger, many of which we see today: deal 'architects' to estimate the liabilities and costs involved in complex services such as outsourcing and specialist lawyers to draw up the contracts. On the buying side, procurement functions developed sophisticated methods of assessing the value of the deals and, although they rarely have the final say in the decision to buy, their counsel was valued given the risks involved in, say, outsourcing a whole function. Organizations grew into the international corporations we know today. As villages become towns and megacities, retail trading relationships become more transactional and pragmatic, less personal and empathic. The same process has occurred in B2B sales.

The digital world has accelerated, depersonalizing B2B trading relationships. Although the travelling sales rep with her coffee supplies for the vending machines on the industrial estate still exists, this type of selling is rapidly disappearing, just as the door-to-door encyclopedia salesperson is the stuff of legend. Why haggle with the rep when you can find the best deal online? It's so embarrassing to say their prices are not competitive, when they have been calling on your business for 20 years. Commodities – whether products or services – are indeed easier to source in this way, but services and solutions – the big deals in B2B trade – are rather different. Anyway, with a product, you can try it, taste it, feel it. Does it do 'what it says on the tin'? Try before you buy. In a world where there is no information asymmetry any more, the role of the salesperson in commodity choice is increasingly redundant; you don't really need help choosing when almost 'perfect' information is available, although you may be spending more time doing the research than you would talking to somebody you trust, who really knows the alternatives and your need.

Business services are different from products. Services – at the point of sale – are promises. Simple services can be tried in advance of purchase, but there is no real guarantee of reliable quality under exceptional circumstances. These promises are not about features; they are about outcomes. These outcomes have benefits, which have to be seen as commensurate with the price charged: a clean office, a well-serviced, reliable fleet of delivery trucks, a performance-enhancing training course. It is difficult sometimes to put a price on such things, as their value is both subjective and objective. The more complex the service, the higher is the risk to the buyer of the outcomes promised and the value not being delivered. At the highest-value end of the service food chain – professional or advisory services like legal, medical, consulting and accountancy – the outcome *has* to be taken on trust. When the delivery of the service may be a unique, one-off event and where the person buying will be materially involved in delivering the outcome with their professional – representation in court, say – there can be no 'try before you buy'. You have to take your in-house counsel's recommendation of the barrister on trust.

'Solutions' – the usual term to describe a tailored bundle of services and products – are no different from services in terms of the risk to customers. Clients can see the software works and play with the hardware involved – this is like buying a product. But the maintenance, the training and the consulting elements are just service promises. When the client signs, she is often putting her own reputation on the line. 'Will the parts of the solution work together – and with what we currently have?' is the first question. Then it's 'Will it deliver the outcomes we need?, then 'Will these outcomes be as valuable as we have been led to believe?', then 'What's the cost – in terms of loss of productivity to introduce, time to train, time to buy, etc.?' The customer needs to have a lot of trust in the vendor and its representatives before they sign.

The challenges of selling B2B

In B2B selling, the ability to build trust is therefore critical. Solutions have to be tailored to client needs at some point, even if they have been designed for specific market sectors. This is because they have to integrate with other solutions working in the business – the legacy of previous buying decisions. As a twenty-first-century B2B salesperson, you had better be good at managing your customer's risks.

Other selling challenges relate to managing the process of client decision-making. When goods and services get packaged up into solutions, they often interfere with the way a business operates. A business school professor might say they 're-engineer the value chain'; a consultant might describe this disruption as 'innovation' but local line managers might be more sceptical. So the decision to buy involves actively accepting this disruption in return for a later benefit – productivity improvement, perhaps, or reduced time to market. Such decisions are generally too risky for one senior manager to make alone. Procurement functions are part of the risk-management process for senior clients; they slow things down (frustrating) but they analyse the risks and benefits of options (reassuring). For the salesperson it means that there are multiple clients involved with different views of their need, the solution, the sort of company they want to work with, the price they want to pay, and so on.

The third challenge is about the calculus between what you, the seller, propose and what each of these stakeholders will use and value. The old model of buying solutions meant that each stakeholder accepted some degree of compromise in the interest of one solution 'sort of' fitting all. All-things-to-all-people solutions are extremely complex and costly. Think of how many of the functions of your computer software you never use (but pay for). Unwanted features and complexity are an irritation in B2B buying, too, an opportunity cost we don't want to pay for. If we can customize our phone, we want to customize our order-processing solution. We don't want to pay an upfront fixed charge for the system, with all the associated depreciation in the value of the asset. If we can pay per use for different vehicles in a city-wide car pool, why shouldn't we pay for our personal usage (heavy or light) of the functions of the solution? The Cloud means that the provider can easily track which functions individuals are using and when, so this is possible to do.

Of course, the information about usage is valuable, not just in terms of billing but also for the client who uses the solution. To know which functions and features people use most, to measure the impact of the outcomes achieved, to be able to modify your business processes on a regular basis to maximize the return – lean processes and lean services – this is a kind of holy grail of management information. Cloud-based solutions have this potential. And the provider, monitoring this information across multiple clients, becomes more intelligent about, say, order processing – to the point where they can really advise their clients about how to do things better, based on real data. The information helps them modify and improve the solution design and may create new revenue streams. The information might be as valuable in some situations as the original solution itself.

The five keys to success

Given this changing environment with increasing customer expectations about convenience and value, what is happening to the selling process? From interviews with successful salespeople, it is clear that new challenges call for some new and some not-so-new responses:

1. You really have to understand your client's business.

This includes the industry, the company's purpose, its business model, its competitive environment and how it competes, its customers and what trends are affecting how and why they buy from your client's company, the pressures it is under, its strategies for growth or survival. You have to be able to talk strategy. You have to anticipate what is going to kill your customer's business and what is going to open new doors. You have to be able to describe outcomes, which your clients will see as valuable, helping them to survive, compete and grow. Many successful salespeople have had previous careers working in industries they now sell into; this is not only about their network of relationships but also about their knowledge and insight from having been there. The solution knowledge is easy to acquire.

2. You have to understand the decision-makers and how they will take a decision to disrupt their business (with your solution).

This is particularly true if your solution completely redesigns the way the client's business operates. Most of the easy productivity gains from computer technology have been won; if a process that used to take the operator two minutes now takes only one, this is not really a productivity gain unless the operator fills the remaining minute doing something more valuable. As a salesperson, you need to be able to assess the impact of your solutions on the current business – structurally, politically, financially and emotionally. You need to provide services and skills to help your client manage this transition or transformation. These skills are organizational as well as technical. You need to gain credibility for the 'new way of doing things' with a wide and diverse audience. You will need a broad network of people within the client organization – and in their industry – who will support your ideas and solutions. You will need to resolve internal power struggles and engage with the client company as a change agent as well as a salesperson.

3. You will need to inspire the organization with your vision.

Selling in the old world promoted the product, showcased it, handled the objections, closed... Today it is more akin to leadership. You are offering to partner with your client for the medium term as they change their organization. (You had better do this anyway, as they won't be paying you a huge up-front sum; the revenues may be spread over a decade.) Where necessary, you will challenge their thinking in a constructive way. You will highlight opportunities they have not foreseen. You have breadth of knowledge and they have depth. You need to present your solution in strategic terms (the concept and how it confers advantage in their market), in technical terms (why it is superior, how it will work with the existing legacy) and in operational terms (how it improves efficiency or reduces risk).

4. You need to build authentic relationships with senior people who will help you meet your quota for years to come.

This means spotting not just needy companies but people whom you can support and sell to over decades, even if they move companies (as they will, if they are the high flyers you need). You need to know yourself and what you can bring to a professional long-term advisory relationship and the sort of client you will work with best. In the solutions world, salespeople are not all pressed out of one mould; they are as different as their clients: commercial extroverts, technical introverts, political fixers. All salespeople are chameleons to some extent, but if you are going to be working with the same clients – even if you and they change companies – then the chemistry piece cannot be fabricated entirely. You will simply not be able to sustain it.

5. Finally – and more invisibly to the client – you will need to have the same sort of relationships internally in *your* company.

You are the guarantee of delivery to your client; if you promise what cannot be delivered, it is your reputation and the trust they placed in you that is diminished. There is really no hiding behind a delivery manager any more. If you don't have strong internal relationships with your own company's technical people who will have to respond to these issues, what you can promise, in terms of tailoring or innovation with the solution basics, will be less. If you always deliver what you promised, you will ensure the renewal or the next sale.

A common feature of all successful B2B salespeople who operate in the digital world is that they have made the transition in their thinking from being interested in their own products to being interested in improving their clients' businesses. They have become genuinely client-centric in their thinking about what they do. One said:

'I don't call myself a salesperson. My job is to help the clients improve what they do. That can mean different things; just listening, coaching, making introductions, giving them new ideas and, yes, proposing solutions. In the real sense of the word, a blend of interventions by our company which will create value for them and – usually – their customers. This is a good place to be. No objections to handle, just tailoring what we have to suit, insofar as we can and they are prepared to pay. Negotiation over price, of course, but within a relationship that has value to both sides. I am selling, but I'm not just a salesperson. I'm their business partner and I often have to fight for their interests internally in my company, which, sadly, talks the talk of "customer first" but walks the talk of quarterly returns.'

This would indicate that, for all the online auctions and solutions jargon, in their hearts and in their heads clients are still much the same as they were when they were wandering the savannah with their flocks 15,000 years ago. They want to know they can trust the salesperson with their daughter as much as with the longer-term health of their business.

1 ENQUIRY BEFORE ADVOCACY

'Judge others by their questions, rather than their answers.'
Voltaire

When you meet clients, the temptation to impress them with what you know, what your company offers, whom you know – and the rest – is very strong. Ask most clients about first impressions and they say that bad salespeople 'talk too much', whereas what impresses them is that they 'asked really good questions'. Expertise is most powerfully demonstrated when it is in the service of the client – in other words, when it is used to frame a good question.

Good questions build relationships and enable you to listen and observe. They indicate that you want to help but on the client's terms. In the solutions world, where outcomes are what clients value, questions reveal this to the salesperson. Armed with the answers, you can write better proposals and price solutions more effectively. All successful salespeople say that good questions are your competitive advantage in the market of people who like to pitch.

ASK QUESTIONS TO ESTABLISH CONTEXT

Here are some favourite opening questions from the sample of successful salespeople interviewed:

- 'I've read the papers but, in your view, how's business? Would you have predicted that answer when you took the job?'
- 'What are the biggest changes you've made over the last 12 months? Were these your choice or a reaction to the environment?'

- 'How have these changes made the company stronger?'
- 'How have your team taken it?'
- 'And you? Sounds quite exciting. Or maybe a bit stressful?'
- 'In your view, where is the company still a bit complacent?'
- 'Why are we having this conversation now (rather than six months ago)? What are the really pressing items on your to-do list?'

Questions about the possibilities for change

Interest in and readiness for change generally have to precede any specific vision of the future and therefore a need for your solution or service. These questions relate to a meeting you have initiated with a target client:

- 'What are your priorities?'
- 'As how important do your colleagues see your list?'
- 'Which do you personally feel most commitment to? Why?'
- 'Which of these are easier and harder to deliver? Why?'
- 'What level of disruption does such a change imply? How keen are people to do that?'
- 'Which company do you envy most? Why? What do you think your company could learn from x?'
- 'What do you see as the missed opportunity here?'
- 'This is a leadership challenge, of course. Where does your company possibly compromise too much?'
- 'What's the 5 per cent here which will deliver the 80 per cent improvement you want?' (Be prepared to answer this yourself.)

Questions to explore the value of change

The value of change is either the problem resolved or the dream achieved, or the difference between the two. As no change is always the easiest option, you start by understanding the motivation:

- 'If this continues unchecked, what are the likely consequences?'
- 'What is the short-term impact of this (problem)? And longer term?' (Explore the financial, political, human, competitive and other sorts of negative impact.)

- 'Are there any silver linings to this cloud? How do you ensure that this (good stuff) happens?'
- 'Under such circumstances, what would success look like to you? Are you sure this isn't a little under-optimistic/too pessimistic?'
- 'If all goes according to plan, what does the company get in return?'
- 'What sorts of outcomes are realistic in the current climate? What sort of financial improvement are you hoping to achieve?'
- 'Is your budget fixed or variable?' ('If it is fixed, tell me and I will tell you if you can afford us and that will save us all time. If it is variable, let's talk about the scope of this project and I will quote you a fair price and you will decide.')
- 'Are you all really brave enough to tackle this?'

ASK QUESTIONS TO EXPLORE THE SOLUTION

The underlying assumption you make in these questions is that the client is both committed and competent. By framing the questions positively, you wait for them to tell you that not everything in the garden is quite as rosy as you might imagine.

- 'Exciting strategies are seldom without risk and I guess you have evaluated them. What are the main ones right now?'
- 'You use words like ["new", "innovative"] to describe what you're planning. This sometimes indicates some gaps in competence or experience. What are you doing to plug any such gaps?'
- 'The company must have undertaken big complex changes like this many times… What has been your experience of how well they do this? What did you learn from the experience?'
- 'Whose heads are on the block over this? Or maybe that's the wrong thing to ask. Who gets the bouquet if this all goes well? How positive are they feeling about this initiative?'
- 'Can you tell me something about the options you have considered for how to do this? Which one did you choose? Why?'
- 'Do you think you will end up compromising, or are the right people brave enough to push through the best option?'

- 'What *don't* you know about this particular change? What difference would it make to have a good answer to that question?'
- 'What might either improve the chances of success or the speed at which you can make the transition?'
- 'Which competitor do you envy?'
- 'I'm sure you have discussed this, but some of this will involve moving into new territory. Which parts of all this may turn out not to be core competencies or processes for your business?'

ASK QUESTIONS TO ENGAGE THEM WITH YOUR SOLUTION

You need to get permission before firing off your expertise or opinions. Possible questions to ask include:

- 'Would you like an outsider's view?'
- 'Can I share some of our experiences in this area?'
- 'We have done some thinking about this whole topic. Would you be interested in hearing some preliminary conclusions?'
- 'A lot of this – particularly some of the dilemmas and decisions you have highlighted – sounds similar to what we encountered on [name project/client]. Can I tell you something about what we have discovered working with other clients on similar themes?'
- 'I guess you must have considered that there might be some advantages to partnering with others on this journey or I wouldn't be here. Is there anything specific in either our communications or what you know about our company that piqued your curiosity?'

Once you have got this permission, your aim is to continue the dialogue. (Imagine you have provided a case study or story about another (anonymized) client or some researched analysis and conclusions.) Again, you do not wish to 'teach' them until or unless they give you the green light:

- 'That was our/my experience. Does this sound anything like what might happen here?'
- 'What do you think of that story?'

- 'Some of this looks relevant to your situation. What do you think?'
- 'Obviously, this is a different company, a different time and one context will never be identical to yours, but is there anything I've said that's relevant to your situation?'

Follow-up

Follow-up is generally a range of actions. The key is to make sure that any action you take is matched by some reciprocal action from them – even if this is only token. This establishes a 'working with' relationship, not the 'working for' relationship associated with product sales. Typical goals will be:

- to secure a follow-up meeting, possibly with other stakeholders – if you think they are really interested (and you have the means), this could be a more formal offer of a workshop to discuss the issue with some experts from your team
- to provide more information – for example, other case studies – with the commitment from them to review these with people who were involved in the situation
- to introduce a specialist who can ask more detailed technical questions – perhaps engaging with the technical people on the client side
- to get a meeting with their boss about the subject.

Questions to get to the next stage

Possible questions to ask include:

- 'I've found this conversation really interesting. I hope you have, too. There are a number of ways we could take this forward...' (Make suggestions.)
- 'If you are interested in this topic – and this is completely without obligation, of course – what would be a good next step? I will send you my notes from this meeting and maybe you could indicate any of your colleagues who might also have a view we should understand in order to see if there may be a way we can assist you with what you are trying to do...'
- 'Where would you like to take this conversation?'

- 'Thank you for your time. I can see some things here we might be able to help you with, but I'm wondering what you think would be a good next step.'
- 'Obviously, we would like to find some area in which we could make a proposal to help you achieve what you want. But at this point I don't have a clear enough idea what that might look like. I can suggest some options if you would like, but usually this is less helpful to people than some other examples and material. If I send you some more targeted material, can we agree a date to discuss this?'

Putting it all together

Questions open up and close down areas of enquiry, but they are more use in relationship-building terms than statements. Although each solution needs a set of questions with which to ascertain the client's potential needs, these may not always be useful in the first meeting.

2 LOGIC OPENS THE MIND, EMOTION OPENS THE WALLET

'If I had asked my customers what they wanted, they would have said a faster horse.'
Henry Ford

The idea that something is good for you – regular exercise, reading *War and Peace* – does not immediately make it desirable. We are rational about what we want to spend our time or money on, but only up to a point, as advertisers and marketeers know well. More basic drives – to be attractive, to be admired for our status – have to be invoked, if you want some people to buy gym membership or copies of Tolstoy's novel. The offer to save you 15 per cent on your car insurance – guaranteed! – is resistible to the consumer because either we don't really need to make the saving (and therefore can't be bothered) or because 15 per cent doesn't sound like a good deal when the premiums go up again after 12 months and the process has to begin again.

In moderately well-run markets for commodity services like banking and energy, consumers do not all shift their business every time there is a better offer, as market investigations by regulators often discover. They conclude that the market isn't working as well as it might, but the complexity of finding out the real information, looking at all the deals (think of telephone tariffs), many of which are market share gainers, not long-term strategic positions, mean that, as consumers, we don't always seek the 'best' deal.

B2B selling, at first sight, is mainly about a reasoned argument for something being good for your company, and this is usually the starting point for most cold calls and marketing activity. 'We have analysed the sales order processing in over 100 companies and found that those who use our solution can experience up to 40 per cent productivity improvements.' But just because we should change our sales order processing doesn't mean we will, because there are other factors that influence our decisions apart from the bottom line.

Advice to buyers represents the process as a rational sequence of actions, something like this:

1. Problem/opportunity recognition
2. Description of the general need
3. Specification of the solution needed
4. Supplier search
5. Request for proposal
6. Supplier selection
7. Performance review
8. Renewal/repeat process again

This rationality is because all organizations have people whose job it is to make Process X competitive and to find ways to improve it. They read articles showing the opportunities; they attend conferences where improvements to quality and cost are routinely discussed; they review ideas in department meetings for changing the way that things are done. But, just as for consumers, they aren't entirely rational in the way they go though the sequence of actions. For example, embedded suppliers are embedded not just because they offer a good deal, but because beds are warm and comfortable and people like to stay in them.

DEMONSTRATE, RATIONALLY, THE OPPORTUNITY FOR CHANGE

To overcome this tendency to conservatism ultimately takes emotion. People have to feel passionately about the alternative, not just accept that rationally it is a good idea.

But it starts with a reasoned argument. Business guru John Kotter said that the first stage of any change was to highlight 'the opportunity for change' but not the specifics of any proposal or vision. This warms people up to the idea that they might be missing out on something wonderful. Note the language: *the opportunity for change*, not *the problem you have*. People need to feel that there is something that they can move towards rather than away from if they are going to persevere. Although we are all to some extent motivated to change things that are wrong, the 'away from' motivation is undirected and once the worst of the problem has been fixed we tend to lose the motivation to change. Losing weight without a target is an example of this. Trying to frighten people into changing never works; they retreat into their shells.

> 'When they ask me to tell them about our business, I start with a brief overview of what we have seen in organizations recently, as it relates to our areas of competence and the services we sell. Everybody loves to know what other people are up to. They are only interested in us insofar as we can be of use to them. I do it in a matter-of-fact sort of way, anonymously about clients, but lots of stats, lots of reassuring evidence that the world is on a journey, but no judgement and not a lot of interpretation. "This is what we find" – that's the message. Depending on the sort of person they are, I tell them about some of the amazing things which our clients are doing too – new products, great campaigns. At some point the client picks up on some fact they find interesting and relate it to their situation, either to highlight that they are better or worse than this position I'm describing. This gets us into specifics. People like specifics, trading numbers. "Why don't people do something about this?" they ask when they are better than most, which means I can pick up on something that they have said and ask the same question.'

It is possible that one client will want exactly what another client has achieved, but unlikely. The value of a solution is about the context as well as the performance, and identical contexts are rare. Focusing on other clients' improvements raises in the client's mind the issue of potentially better outcomes for their business, in their context. Their reason tells them 'We could do this better, faster, cheaper than we do now' and this starts them thinking about how and with whom.

FIND OUT WHO ELSE SEES THINGS THE SAME WAY

The link between the possibility and a solution they will pay for lies in people, not in product. Salespeople know that any solution of any complexity will involve a range of decision-makers, sponsors and stakeholders. To achieve this will require support – or your prospect, no matter how enthused, may be marginalized by less enthused stakeholders.

A key question when the client seems interested is 'Who else might see this as an opportunity?' Marshalling the forces of a group of interested people is a change leadership strategy that works well for salespeople, too. Providing a workshop facilitator from your organization to discuss ideas might be a good next step. Show the interested members of the department some alternative futures and discuss them. Highlight the change issues related to some of these choices. They know that you are selling, but they can also recognize that you are helping.

'The consultative sell is really what you have to do. Because they can find out everything on the Internet or from talking with colleagues in other companies, there isn't much chance of blagging anybody any more. You have to be prepared to discover that your solution isn't right for them and that you have wasted your time. Except you haven't. You just had access to a whole IT department, which would have taken you months of cold-calling. You should be able to make something out of that, surely?'

EXCITE THEM WITH A VISION, ONE YOU CO-CREATE

If there is a constituency of agreement about the general opportunity, the group can then – with your help – move to defining more precisely what that vision of loveliness might actually look like. There are many opportunities to bring in specialists of all sorts from your company to help their specialists with their thinking; what's possible, what others are doing, what's a waste of time in practice, the 20 per cent that delivers the 80 per cent of the value. They might prefer to hire consultants to do this, being 'solution-agnostic', as if consultants really were. Consultants who benchmark options for the client will be contacting their network anyway, so this may or may not be that objective. The complete list of suppliers might not 'play ball' with the consultants. You are more likely to know about the competition in the space than consultants, as you go up against them every day...

It all comes back to trust, again.

It is the vision that makes them think about spending money. When they all have some emotional engagement, they will be more likely to look for the budget. When collectively they feel excited by what they might be about to do, when they have a goal that quickens the pulse, they are more likely to advocate change within the company and the company is more likely to respond with some cash.

Putting it all together

Deciding to institute a change is both a rational and an emotional process:

- From the rational perspective, we analyse, we think differently, then make a change.
- From the emotional perspective, we see, we feel differently, then make a change.

The process starts with a rational appraisal of the opportunity for beneficial change; no clear solution, just analysis of a hunch or an idea. When this is confirmed, an interested group starts working on a more precise vision of what that change might look and feel like. From this emerges the desire to change in a particular direction... and the case for funding.

If you sell solutions, you are selling change, and the use of these two aspects of organizations needs to be managed carefully. The old model of introducing a new system and forcing people to change their behaviour as a result only really works quickly when the commitment to use the system and change the behaviour has occurred before it is introduced. The desire to change is an emotional acceptance of a future state. It helps to have been part of designing it.

3 IT'S WORTH WHAT CLIENTS BELIEVE

*'Because it is hard for a competitor to offer the full spectrum
of capabilities comprising a well-designed solution bundle,
it's much easier to protect premium pricing in a solution sale
than in a traditional product sale.'*
Dixon and Adamson

If value in B2B trades is principally about outcomes such as
increasing revenues, lowering costs and reducing risks, you would
imagine that the client's perception of value would be a rational
one. You could indeed present a cost comparison between your
solution and what an identical outcome is currently costing the
client, and the demonstrated saving would be a logical way to
present the value of what you offer. You could also compare the
costs and benefits of your solution with others in the market. You
might perhaps demonstrate additional benefits such as time savings
and quality improvements, which are possible because of the larger
volumes your company would be processing for the client.

But despite such calculations – which are important in assessing
how much the client might reasonably be expected to pay – the
real judgement is about the value-in-use of your service, and the
less tangible outcomes that your solution or service produces.
These assessments are influenced by perceptions of the value
of political influence, enhanced reputation, increased trust in
the team, customer satisfaction, perceived or actual scarcity,
brand value, aesthetics, convenience to users and many other
aspects. Many of these assessments are situational and about
relationships as well as hard numbers.

After the event, clients recognize this. What do you most hope to
hear when you return to see clients and check how the solution is
delivering? 'You are expensive but good value for money.' When
you do these reviews, you learn what people really value, which
can be different from what the solution delivers.

A salesman who had been a project manager recalled a client's perception of value, after the project was over:

'The consulting project we did which helped Ford to produce the first globally sourced motor car – the Mondeo in Europe and other models elsewhere – was designed to save the company billions of dollars over the lifetime of the car. Mind you, the fees were substantial – one of the biggest consulting projects we ever did. After the two-year project was over, the partner and I were collecting feedback by interviewing client members of the team. We asked the standard question, "What did we do that really added value on this project?" to all the clients involved, from the vice-president to co-opted team members. Bob – a Ford lifetime buyer approaching retirement – who had been with the project throughout and seen it all, said; "Shoot, that's a hard one..." He thought a bit and then said, "You remember that time we were waiting outside the boardroom in Dearborn and I was about to do my first presentation to the board? I was really nervous, although you had prepared us well. But you just sat there and talked calmly and sorta held our hand before we went in. That I will always remember. That was valuable." I couldn't remember the moment at all; it must have been spontaneous. Billions saved, but this was what value meant to him.'

'Good value for money' means different things to different people and the bottom-line benefits must be there – your solution must do what it says on the tin. But for most clients it is the realization that you are responsive, easy to do business with, considerate and sensitive of their situation that creates the recognition of that value.

Perceived value is about the situation as well as your solution.

ASK STAKEHOLDERS TO DESCRIBE WHAT SUCCESS LOOKS AND FEELS LIKE

It is well known in market research that consumers cannot describe a solution or product to fill a gap they are unaware of. No focus group could have dreamed up the iPod. But when they are shown a new product, customers will give a view. The same process may be relevant to clients considering solutions with which they are unfamiliar. Often, the proposal drafting process does this in terms of what the new good might look like, but the exploration may not go far enough.

When you have defined the performance criteria for the solution – the best commercial option – you need to find out about your client's 'value context' – what aspects of the change they would value. You need to ask stakeholders more about:

- how they feel now about what they currently have
- what success or 'better' looks like
- how this changed state would make them and others feel
- how this changed state would be different from what they have now
- how you can help them get the 'best of both worlds'.

Your aim is to open up their thinking about the future as well as to understand what they value (and what they don't) about your solution and its implementation. Some will list the bottom-line effects and others will either underplay them or not mention them at all.

Furthermore

If you need a structure to collect these ideas, it is helpful to think of comparing these answers with the standard list of generic benefits, with the acronym SPACED: safety, performance, appearance, convenience/comfort, dependability/durability.

WORK OUT WHICH 'SOFT' ASPECTS OF THE CHANGE ARE LIKELY TO BE MOST VALUED

When you have lists of 'must haves' and 'nice to haves', you will need to prioritize these and integrate them into your proposal. Here are some valued aspects of change to consider. (They will not be valued by everyone and not everybody will experience them.)

- New skills to learn
- Different people to interact with
- Fresh challenges
- More control over my time
- New ways of thinking
- Less routine work – more problem-solving
- Better use of my existing skills
- Enhanced status or reputation
- New beginnings; the chance to reinvent myself
- New opportunities

Some solutions providers carry out this sort of work only when the contract has been signed, as a means to identify potential barriers to acceptance and to think about how best to plan the implementation. Exploring the other 'wins' from your solution might differentiate you in the eyes of the customers and also demonstrate your commitment to helping them make the best of the situation.

SHAPE YOUR SOLUTION TO REFLECT THESE ASPECTS OF VALUE

When IBM became a global services company in the 1990s, many of the services that are now charged for were given away free with the large computers they sold. Services like training in the use of new systems were known as the 'gift wrapping' and salespeople did not consider the cost (or the value) of these 'add-ons' and their outcomes. For the clients themselves, however, there was little point in having an expensive computer that nobody was ready to use, so this perception of value was almost overlooked; at the outset IBM was a technology company with good client relationships, but not a services company.

Although this would never happen now – people are much more aware of how the context shapes customer perceptions of value – some traces of this sort of thinking remain, particularly in companies providing highly engineered solutions. If your delivery team is dominated by the functional or commercial perception of value alone, they may miss a very real opportunity to add more value and get another sale. When you look at what aspects of a solution people *use*, it is different from what aspects of the solution people *like* and *value*.

Putting it all together

As solutions are flexible, you can adapt them to the customer's 'value context'. This will materially influence the value perception of your solution-in-use. Exploring this aspect of the sales process will not only help you to tailor the solution but will also enhance the value – and the price a client may be prepared to pay.

At first sight, it is the economic value of the solution that appeals to customers; that is what starts the process of investigation of alternatives. But retrospectively these things are not as important to people's perceptions of value. What was the original rationale becomes a hygiene factor, something that is a baseline for expectation. It is the promise of delivering not only the economic but also the human outcomes that will enable you to deliver a solution that is 'reassuringly expensive'.

4 BIG OCCASIONS PROMPT BIG SPENDING

'As long as you aren't selling, people will talk to you.'
Jeff Thull

In retail, shopkeepers emphasize events like Back to School and Valentine's Day, as a way to stimulate sales. Weddings are a licence for every service provider to charge high prices; nobody wants to be seen to be skimping on their big day. I had never thought about the impact of big events on B2B sales until a partner in a consulting firm pointed out the similarity:

> 'Big events for clients include being promoted, especially if your new job puts you in charge of a larger budget, moving to a new company, taking on your first really senior managerial job. The reason is simple: when clients get new opportunities at work they are expected to change things. They may even have been hired precisely for this reason.'

Serendipity apart, this means you should be selective about the clients whose careers you track. You will also probably encourage or help them to find new jobs from time to time out of enlightened self-interest; they may repay you with a project.

DON'T EXPECT IMMEDIATE BUYING SIGNALS

Assuming that there isn't a crisis, most clients observe the '90-day rule' when moving jobs: this means not changing anything but just watching, listening and waiting for the first three months. Then they go to their new boss (or the board) with their assessment of the situation and some outline proposals for things they want to do. At the same time, they may need to indicate both the costs and the benefits of making these changes.

This suggests that the salesperson whose client moves up or to another job should be having conversations and perhaps preparing ideas and rough estimates during these 90 days, but not expect to sell anything for at least another 90 – six months after the client moves. This is a period in which many clients will be very open to being helped by a person they know, so this first period is a chance for you to build up goodwill in the relationship, even if there is no business in the short term. If you wait until they have done their analysis, you will be one of many picking up a request for proposal (RFP) rather than influencing the content, or even making a non-competitive bid.

KEEP IT AS LOW KEY AS THEY WOULD LIKE

A new job is like nectar to those worker bees, the sales community; everybody wants to meet the new boss, especially those who realize that their current contracts might be at risk now that someone new is in charge. You may have been one of these account managers who has to 'update' the new arrival on the success of the current project or contract. Most new managers take this information with a pinch of salt as they know the vendor has to resell when the old sponsor leaves; they will probably rely more on their own team to help them decide what to do, except that they don't really know whether to trust the judgement of their new team either.

So it is important to play it cool. Of course, contact them immediately you hear the news – not just from LinkedIn. Send congratulations. Offer support. Arrange a lunch somewhere near their new office after about four weeks. Send the client information that might be of interest to their new role. *Don't try to sell them anything.* (Everybody else is doing that.) Focus on the relationship. Usually, your aim is to help them make good decisions about both current and future solutions. In most cases, their hands will be tied by existing contracts, but advance warning of renewals or their thinking about what needs to change can give you some advantage. Your position as their adviser is substantiated if you try to help them only with things that your company provides and then act with generosity to some of your incumbent competitors, as appropriate. As they are reinventing themselves, so can you.

The client will know you from what you have delivered before, so you will need to make sure that they potentially know about other solutions your company provides, more relevant to their new job. Offer this information only when they have given you some facts about the situation they find themselves in – and only if it is in their best interests. Remember, they need to impress their new boss and their team. The biggest mistake at this point in their career would be to make a wrong decision; and that includes buying something from you that is not what they need.

AND IF THE CLIENT IS FIRED OR MADE REDUNDANT...

Getting fired is a big event in anybody's book. Good clients feel the heat more than the average as they progress up the corporate ladder; there's more competition, more envy and more aggressive behaviour, if you are a star. If the client is ambitious as well as talented, they will be pushing themselves and they may make the odd false move along the way. This means that high-profile, talented clients can expect to have a bad experience at least once.

How you react as the salesperson on the account is important, as this is actually a medium-term opportunity. In the short term, it can be a crisis for existing business.

First, you will want to secure any current contracts sponsored by the person leaving. If you have a good relationship and they are not marched out of the office, then they will want to do the same and protect their legacy, as far as they can. (With promotions this is easier to manage, as there will be a notice period and a chance for you to work with their successor.) This assumes that they are leaving on good terms with their boss, but on the occasions where they are not, the supplier and account manager are often well placed to support the company and 'fill the gap'.

Secondly, if they are good but unlucky, as I have suggested, they will end up somewhere else fairly soon. (Let's hope they don't want you to find them a job in *your* company...) If your company organizes sales relationships by account rather than on an individual basis, you may have a problem maintaining the relationship when they leave, especially if they end up in another company not on your target list. The opportunity is to get them to 'take you with them' to whichever company they work for next. This will happen if you demonstrate that you believe in them as clients by continuing to stay in touch while they are looking for another job, on gardening leave or whatever the hiatus turns out to look like. 'A friend in need is a friend indeed.'

Doing the opposite – dropping them like a hot coal when they lose their job – will have the opposite effect and you will be seen as just a 'fair-weather friend'. This is worth pointing out to your boss, who may think that your job is to build a relationship with their replacement. It is, but it is also to track the original client if they are talented.

Putting it all together

Big career events are opportunities if you handle them well. New jobs create needs for change and that in turn creates the need for services and solutions.

Clients will generally be loyal if you stay loyal to them. If your behaviour demonstrates that you are interested only in the short-term maintenance of the current contracts, they will drop you, too. The salesperson who supports their client through a crisis or transition will usually be rewarded at some point.

5 TO CHANGE IS TO LOSE

'People don't resist change; they resist being changed.'
Peter Senge

When a client is doing badly, they are open to solutions. To a drowning man even a straw looks appealing. The client may lack the means to pay for the solution they need, but that is another matter. When a client business is roaring away, they are less open to changing the recipe. The current recipe seems to be working, so why would they?

High-performing businesses feel they have more to lose by changing than underperforming ones. Logically, this makes sense in terms of risk, but not in terms of innovation and any company's need to reinvent itself. All companies have to make changes continuously to stay afloat, and to lead the pack they need to innovate and learn faster than their competitors. As management consultant Reg Revans suggested, in successful organizations the rate of learning has to equal or be greater than the rate of change to which they are subject.

That is not how it feels. Leaving the known for the unknown is experienced as a potential loss by everybody involved. It is one of the major barriers to selling solutions which transform companies.

All clients experience change as loss.

TO CHANGE, CLIENTS HAVE TO ADMIT TO COMPLACENCY AT BEST AND IGNORANCE AT WORST

Clients have built careers on their approach to managing a process or a business unit. They are psychologically invested in that approach because it has brought them success. Although they may know that success breeds complacency and that winning formulae need reviewing and revising, they experience this as a loss. Some clients are more prone to conservative thinking than others, because openness to change is an aspect of personality. But everybody dislikes the thought of generational shift: their great project consigned to the trashcan of history. Their legacy will be forgotten, and with it a part of them.

Perhaps for this reason, there are very few cases of companies remaining successful over many generations. Although this is good news for entrepreneurs, it is less good news perhaps for institutional shareholders who would like secure returns over longer terms. Identifying areas of complacency, where the leading player is not actually the leader, can be a difficult task, although the incentive to remain as number one can be useful for the salesperson trying to find these holes in the client's armour.

Be careful about what you say. As one salesman expressed it, 'Never call your client's baby ugly, even if it is.' The only way to tackle this is using language that reflects:

- continuity of excellence ('best in class solution')
- convenience (ideas that will save you time or effort)
- the cross-pollination of ideas ('They have got some interesting ways of dealing with this in the insurance industry').

Attempts to criticize the client's current approach when things are looking rosy will result in denial, anger or worse.

IF YOU CHANGE, YOU MAY LOSE POWER AND STATUS

The plethora of change initiatives in many organizations indicates many things, not all of them good. I have known boards of directors sponsoring more than six major projects at the same time, mostly without any knowledge of the others or their interrelationships. Sponsoring projects raises your status and it is easier to start new ones than admit a project is a waste of money and cancel it. Change proliferates but this doesn't make it happen faster.

On the surface – and in the annual report – all these projects can show that management is aware of the need to keep up with the times, but they could also indicate that senior managers hedge their bets. I remember asking a senior HR executive working as part of a joint consultant/client team why he had been unable to attend the recent monthly meetings. It was an innocent question but he looked at me rather suspiciously. 'I'm involved in a number of these projects, you know,' he said rather shamefacedly. How many? 'Six.' Given that this project was to revise the whole retail proposition of a bank, I was surprised and my face showed it. 'They don't always work out, you know,' was his retort. Clearly, he thought our project was toast. (It was.) In companies that are as over-consulted and over-solutionized as many of the financial services firms in the world, the natural tendency is to protect your own position, because somebody else's project might lead to your demotion or even your demise. Great performance is no guarantee of job security where everybody is on the steering committee of six transformational projects.

This is a hard fact of life for salespeople to combat in order to sell beneficial solutions. People are battle-hardened and resistant to any form of change on principle, as change is always a threat to their position. The most common approach is to try to get in at the highest possible level for the sponsorship of your project or service. If your client calls the shots, he can control the others and his power will be secured. Clients can be tempted by projects simply to defend their position.

This is dangerous because the value of the project is purely political and it can be dumped unceremoniously if the person loses some corporate battle and is fired. While salespeople cannot guarantee that nobody loses out in solutions, it is important to think about how this will be communicated to stakeholders.

MAKE SURE YOU ARE EQUIPPED TO DEAL WITH THE NEW WORLD (AND THAT YOU WANT IT)

New solutions and changing working practices demand new skills. It is part of the acceptance process to offer help and skill development for those whose competence is threatened by what you propose.

Even if you do so, there will be some people who feel that this is one change too many and they may block the idea. Using Facebook on company time? Those who can't wouldn't sanction the idea. Those who know that the information is vital for marketing and selling would disagree, but you would have to know its value to approve its use. The basic technique is to create some powerful ambassadors for the acquisition of the new skills, particularly for stakeholders who might be assumed to be the most resistant. If they can learn to operate within the solution, surely so can anybody?

Putting it all together

Understanding the different senses of loss, which any major change involves, is the start of getting broad acceptance. While you cannot avoid these losses, you can be sympathetic to how people feel about them, while highlighting the necessity to stay ahead, modernize and compete.

Including practical steps to reduce the sense of loss in your proposals will help – for example, training people in new skills – but in the end such losses may be part of the company investment in staying ahead.

6 OPPORTUNITIES ARE MORE ATTRACTIVE THAN PROBLEMS

'We cannot solve our problems with the same thinking we used when we created them.'
Albert Einstein

Every customer is conditioned by their habitual way of seeing both problems and opportunities. This 'known' world of possibility is, to the rational mind, limited, as Einstein observed. But precisely because it *is* familiar it influences the holder of that view; it seems safer than it is. Over time all organizations tend to entropy and its emotional cellmate, complacency.

Clients who 'already have the answer' tend to reject sales calls, just as they reject change. The challenge is – when you get in front of them – to 'unfreeze' the customer's perception, shake their company's complacency. If you do this too fast or too furiously, the client feels judged or even threatened and will retreat behind the castle walls of their experience and the way of seeing that lies within the keep. It takes subtlety and a creative idea to capture the client's interest. Reframing makes the possibility of change neutral – a chance to discuss and open up the assumptions that determine the client's self-diagnosis.

Reframing simply means changing the assumptions about the information you have on the client's issue and presenting it in a different way. When did the 'tourism industry' become the 'leisure business'? Nobody quite remembers. When did railways stop thinking of people as 'passengers' – items of freight to be shipped carefully – and start to think of them as 'customers'? Shifting a self-perception of an issue, or a whole business, is something only the outsider can do, because they do not share the same assumptions. Does your customer 'make lipstick' or are they in the 'beauty business'? It depends on whom you ask.

When the customer is given a different idea about their problem (or their solution in mind), when they hear different words used to describe the familiar, they start to think about it in a different way.

- First, they become more aware of their assumptions, because here, sitting in their office, is somebody with different assumptions who comes up with a contrary view. (There is a good reason why strategy consultants tend to be of a different generation from their board-level clients...)
- Secondly, the customer may like the new formulation and see it as a legitimate alternative, one that others might find interesting, or that would at least provoke some beneficial discussion. For this reason alone some clients will pay attention.
- Thirdly, a new way of looking creates new ways out of the situation for people who are 'stuck'. They feel negative because they are stuck. Often, their habitual way of seeing things is limited; people who live in the forest can't easily see the wood for the trees and they know this.

Here are some options to consider when discussing a problem that you want to reframe.

CHANGE THE LEVEL OF PROBLEM DEFINITION

Your client will see the world through the lens of their own job – whether it is operations, managerial, technical, strategic or executive. You see the problem through the lens of your solution or competence. Before presenting *your* perception of the problems, you need to create alternatives that might make sense to your customer.

Once, when training consultants on this topic in a large computing company, we were discussing how to get the client to agree the scope of the work. I suggested inviting them to list the questions they wanted the project to address. A guy – 20 years in the company, at least – put up his hand and said, 'Jeremy, I'm not sure you get what our business is really about. It doesn't matter what the client's question is, the answer is always the MP5000 [the most expensive product on their list].' The room laughed; this was the way most of them had learned to deal with client questions in a product world. In the service world they were entering, they needed to reframe the idea of using questions.

Here are some ways to reframe a problem:

1. **Zoom out:** raise the level at which the problem is defined, making it more abstract and strategic (e.g. unit cost reduction becomes 'efficiency metrics', operational problems become 'competitive weaknesses').
2. **Zoom in:** lower the level at which the problem is defined (e.g. from supply-chain strategy to choice of supplier, from regional management policy to individual plant manager competence).
3. **Flip the problem:** turn it on its head (e.g. from cost reduction to sustainable growth, from lack of resources to inability to agree priorities).
4. **Change position:** go upstream or downstream in the value chain (e.g. not design but sales, not operations but customer relationship management).
5. **Name the 'elephant in the room'** (e.g. you have no real process for board decision-making now the boss has left) – but do this carefully so as not to appear critical of the client.

How you express this will depend on the situation and your solution. Short tropes are useful sometimes, to reset the client's view of the scope of their need. I worked with a very good salesperson in a business that helped organizations improve customer service. At some point in the conversation he would introduce a tangential idea: 'Yes, but how you manage is actually how they serve.' Suddenly, the operational problem had been laid at the door of the executives and their behaviour. If you can work up some similar thoughts that divert the original presentation of the problem and make it one that affects the person in front of you (and one your solution is designed to address), you may get to a more engaging conversation sooner.

CONFRONT THE CUSTOMER'S ASSUMPTIONS ABOUT THE SOLUTION WITH NEW IDEAS

All clients have ideas about what solution they need. They have usually discussed ideas internally before they contact providers, or when the process of selling has alerted them to the possibility of improvement. The process of exploration and learning happens in parallel with the process of creating a clear set of principles about 'what would work here'. These may be more or less fixed as ideas, depending on the client and their situation.

Salespeople are usually more experienced at reframing the customers' solutions-in-mind than they are at redirecting their thinking about the problem. Reframing solutions requires you to understand your client's (implicit or explicit) acceptance criteria and then interpose different ones.

'Acceptance criteria' are not the same as 'outcomes delivered'. They relate to:

- timing (available now)
- duration of implementation
- scope of impact
- visibility of impact (reputation)
- risk (which may relate to any of the above)
- cost.

One way to uncover your client's acceptance criteria is to invite them to describe their 'ideal' solution. (Depending on their experience, you can end up with a wish list of criteria – such as zero risk, instantaneous commercial impact everywhere and huge credibility for them in the company – for virtually no cost.) Then ask them what is likely to be acceptable in the wider company.

Another way is to get them to share their vision of how they would like things to look in the future; clients sometimes enjoy the exercise of freewheeling about how things could change. Afterwards, you can ask, 'What trade-offs are you prepared to make for this to happen in the real world?' You might also ask, 'What solutions are you *not* prepared to consider?'

If you play back the assumptions underlying your client's acceptance criteria, you are starting the process of reframing their idea about the solution. Where they say 'risk', you ask about 'return'. Where they use 'cost', you might say 'investment'. If, in answer to questioning their preferred approach to change, they say 'evolutionary', you might say 'Why not revolutionary?' Challenging their ideas helps them understand their assumptions, and also alerts them to the fact that their thinking *is* assumptive.

The most powerful way to get clients to see solutions in a different way is to give them a first-hand experience of an alternative. Take them to meet people who are using your solution on a daily basis, or who have benefited from your service. Customers' habitual ways of thinking about a solution are based on their repeated experience, not reason. Seeing, feeling and touching an alternative address the process by which underlying assumptions are formed and provide new experience. For many, this will do more to change their thinking than pages of numbers. Why? Because a) your suggestions are real and b) people use them and they appear to work.

PRESENT A FEW ALTERNATIVES

Predicate your discussion of other ways of seeing problems and solutions with a comment on the client: 'You're a [creative] person, I think, so I hope you will find a couple of other ways of looking at what you told us last time for an interesting input to your situation.' Positively labelling your client before you show the alternatives prepares them for what is to come and helps to make them responsive, rather than seeing your alternatives as a judgement on what they have said.

Generally, fewer alternatives encourage choice and therefore buy-in (and, with any luck, buying). When reframing the problem, the number of options you present depends on how you reckon your influence with the person. One reframing is often enough if you know the person well; for a new client, three alternatives should be the maximum.

Putting it all together

Questioning effectiveness usually precedes discussing efficiency. The question 'Are you shooting at the right target?' should always be resolved before asking 'Are you using the correct weapon?' In other words, until the problem is clarified, discussing the solution may be premature. Clients always feel their own diagnosis is good – or they wouldn't issues RFPs.

But if your solution doesn't fit their definition of the problem, you will have a hard time selling to them unless you are allowed to reframe the problem. That permission is often about making sure they don't feel judged.

7 COMPETITION HELPS

'Competition is always a good thing. It forces us to do our best. A monopoly renders people complacent and satisfied with mediocrity.'

Nancy Pearsey

In theory, salespeople like to avoid competitive bids because these force down the price they can charge. But if you are a market leader, competition prevents smugness and keeps you focused on the reality of what clients really value.

Most salespeople enjoy the thrill of the campaign more when they know there is competition. Good salespeople like to win, and if there is no serious competition then victory can taste less sweet.

'We always compare ourselves with x (the market leader) and often go up against them. They are the big guy and we play the underdog, so nipping at their heels is often all we can manage. But we always want the chance, because we know that only by competing can we really learn to do what they do and do it better than them. We are cheaper and in many ways offer better value, but clients mostly play safe, so we need to find ways to reassure them. We are targeting their clients with small bids to get a track record. If *their* clients say *we* are great, what's the risk?'

DECIDE WHAT MAKES YOU DIFFERENT

Competition makes you focus on your difference. Are you smaller? More agile and responsive? New to the market? Fresh ideas and loads of energy? Technically inferior? Do you provide the important functions without the noise of whistles and bells that just distract people?

'We aren't the biggest, or anything like the biggest, but that keeps us on our toes. We really want your business and will show you what it means to us. We wouldn't all have left comfortable jobs in other better-established firms if we didn't know there was an opportunity to add far more value than them. We are proud of what we have achieved and know that what we can achieve for you will make you proud as well.'

I'm talking with a very good salesperson who has just gone out on his own with three others. They are on a mission and he is answering my question about how you cope with competition as the new kid on the block.

'I never apologise for anything. Why should I? What did Disraeli say? "Never complain or explain." If they don't want to take a bit of a chance on us, they probably aren't the right sort of client anyway. We can only be leading edge if clients allow us to be. I have seen a load of start-ups whose bright ideas foundered on the mediocrity of building a reputation for doing one thing brilliantly. They just went on and on doing that thing until it wasn't brilliant any more. Flawless mediocrity. We have to avoid that.'

Many start-ups define themselves in opposition to the bigger companies, by saying that they are not like them. This is a good story at the start, but later they find they have to be able to articulate a more robust proposition about themselves and what they are going to build as a business. Knowing what makes you different turns into what will make you succeed. When the start-up phase is over, you need to be able to articulate how your vision is different as well.

USE COMPETITION TO FORCE YOU TO GIVE SUPERIOR SERVICE

There is often less difference between solutions than salespeople would like the client to believe. If solutions have been designed for a particular market need, their functions are often broadly similar, just as software does similar things for functions like word processing. The interface may be different, the way your solution integrates may be different, but often the major difference between several similar solutions is in the service you provide.

The best reputation for growth attracts the best staff, who in turn delight the customers who provide the basis for that growth, or so the virtuous circle of performance improvement suggests. Competition for clients is often about service in retail and leisure purchasing, as well as price. A hotel that offers superior service often scores better than one with superior facilities, as the experience of a hotel is as much about hospitality as the number of rooms. In the same way, smaller companies often compete with larger ones in terms of a more personal service; indeed, they *have* to compete based on this unless they have some proprietary technology or element to their solution that makes them the 'must have' option for customers.

So, all other things being equal, responsiveness, going the extra mile, anticipating client needs, tailoring what you do to what they really want, offering better value unprompted by highlighting some useful feature the client has overlooked, responding positively to complaints, welcoming feedback, matching what competitors provide for less... all these signs of good service, provoked by competition, can give you advantages over the features of competitors' solutions – particularly if your solution involves major change.

As one salesperson said, 'You can improve the functionality of the solution far more easily, but more expensively, than you can the caring function in your staff. That niceness is something you have to recruit for.'

COMPETING MAKES SELLING MORE ENJOYABLE AND CLIENTS MORE COMMITTED

At first sight, this might sound odd because the aim of a great salesperson is often to create a non-competitive situation. But if selling were *never* competitive it would be rather dull. Imagine a game of tennis where neither party really wanted to win.

The odds have to be right, however, for selling competitively to be motivating. In some tendering processes there is a need to show that a large field of potential suppliers has been considered and, in the case of some government work, that they represent different segments of the market. Sometimes you will be invited to bid where there is already an incumbent supplier who can easily meet the need for the solution and you wonder why you are on the list. When you are a 'make weight' bidder, the effect of competition is negative. 'You have to bid, of course, or your company is "off the list" in future', as one salesperson expressed it. 'But if we have intelligence that this isn't real competition, then we do a cut-and-paste job on the proposal.'

In some situations, competition encourages the client to make a stronger commitment to the winner. For this reason, if client commitment is critical to the success of your solution, salespeople may actually suggest that clients scan the field before making a decision. One successful executive coach – who sells all her own work – told me that she always asks a potential client who else they are talking to. If the answer is no one, she tells them that coaching is a personal choice and the chemistry has to be correct, so they should look more broadly. 'Generally, it works in my favour, because it demonstrates that I really want the best for them.'

Putting it all together

Competing technically can require large amounts of investment, but the human aspect of being either smaller or more nimble can play to your advantage. If courtesy costs nothing, service does, but it requires a little investment for you to compete. Well-recruited people who like their clients' businesses to succeed, who are socially adept as well as technically savvy, can make a huge difference. Competition makes you confront this aspect of your proposition to the client. If this is the case, good.

8 REASONABLE PRICES ARE RELATIVE PRICES

*'A $7,000 bag makes a similar $2,000 bag more desirable.
(It is so much less expensive and it's still got the designer
label.) This results in increases in sales of the $2,000 bags –
which might otherwise have been rejected as too expensive,
too wilfully over the top...'*
William Poundstone

If value relates to context and pricing is, in part, your decision
about the market positioning of your brand, customers'
perception about what is *reasonable* to pay is relative to other
experience of prices. What are this client's reference points about
price? What does your customer expect to have to pay? How do
you know?

If you think of your own negative experiences, a 'rip-off' price
is a sum that equates neither to value nor to other prices known
to you, the customer. It is often a complaint about one-off events
aimed at families – Christmas Wonderlands, pop-up theme parks,
wilderness experiences – or about services, which people pay
for only infrequently – re-asphalting the drive, fixing the roof –
where they have little idea about the true costs or comparative
prices. After the event they realize that, compared to what the
neighbours paid, the experience and/or the driveway was tacky.
Next time, we check the market rate.

Although these are B2C examples, price relativity affects what
people equate to a sum being 'reasonable to charge' in B2B
situations, too. A bad experience of unfair pricing may put the
customer off a similar purchase for a long time, just as a positive
experience may encourage them to trust the price proposed.

In B2B situations there are a number of relativities at play in how customers perceive price 'reasonableness':

- **Your quoted price relative to other options in the market**

If you are at the top end, clients will expect more and vice versa at the bottom. At both the top and bottom end of the price scale, clients have to convince themselves that either you are worth the premium or the lower price is worth the risk. Clients tend to choose higher-than-average-priced solutions to balance out these factors. Clients rarely choose the cheapest option unless other factors make them certain about managing any risks, for example a repeat purchase from a trusted supplier who is discounting to keep the business.

- **Your quoted price compared with the amount of money they feel they *have* to spend or invest**

Clients will have done their own research before starting down the road of hiring any service provider or vendor and will have thought about a 'budget', even if they have completed only a minimum of research. If your charges are in line with this expectation, price will not be the issue.

- **Your quoted price relative to what they have spent in the past (sometimes a long time ago)**

Experienced customers have a different view from first-timers. (Procurement people are often positioned as the most 'experienced', as buying things at a reasonable price is their job. This only really works with categories of frequently bought commodities, not solutions.) When a customer is renewing a contract they will assume that the renewal cost should be no more than last time plus inflation, but might feel that, if during the first cycle you had set-up costs, the repeat price should be lower. When quoting renewal prices it is therefore important to emphasize innovations – the additional features and benefits based on the previous experience. They can help legitimize a price rise above inflation.

OFFER AND SELL THE 'BIG TICKET' ITEMS FIRST

Salespeople in stores know that the customer buying the suit should be shown the most expensive suits first (anything less might be insulting to that badly dressed millionaire). Then, when the customer has selected a suit, you may try to sell them a shirt, tie and cufflinks in that order (as the cost of the cufflinks compared to the rest of the purchase is small – even if the margin on cufflinks is higher than on other items). Customers may then ask for a discount for the 'package' but the 10 per cent offered is still worth it for the store.

In B2B situations, adding more to the bundle may not make your offer more persuasive, as any user of software will acknowledge. A study where people were offered a choice between gym membership and a home gym found that people were divided approximately 50/50 in their choice. When a fitness DVD was added to the home gym option, customers' choices for the gym membership rose by 31 per cent. It seems that customers work out the rough averages of items that they buy, not the incremental added value of each element.

As this relates to selling B2B, it suggests that the total figure you quote can be presented in proposals in very different ways, but that you should start by setting out the 'basic' price and that this price should be the most expensive component of the solution. If you can get agreement to the 'big ticket' element of the spend, irrespective of the payment terms, you have then created a basic price against which other elements will be favourably compared. 'More' is not necessarily as attractive as 'more fit for purpose'.

CREATE A HIGH-PRICED OPTION TO HELP CLIENTS SEE YOUR MID-PRICE OPTION AS BETTER VALUE

An alternative to this is to create an extremely elaborate, zero-risk, high-profile, copper-bottomed option, which has elements that are, in the customer's terms, 'unreasonably' priced because it is unreasonably cautious, over-designed or over-engineered and monitored. This 'gold standard' of the sort of solution the client needs is exactly that: a benchmark for all other options.

The real option – the one which will provide the outcomes they want and you with the margin you need – is the second-choice option. Restaurants sell more rump and fillet steak than

Chateaubriand (for two), but the existence of the mega-steak option makes the price of the others seem reasonable. In the same way, you draw attention to the second option by starting with something excessive. You can offer more than two 'second options' in terms of prices which are reasonably close to each other.

If you provide a stripped-back 'bargain basement' offer, be prepared for clients to try to build up from this to reach the mid-range option at a lower price. Never present lower prices without highlighting the potential disadvantages (risks, time taken, requirement for extensive participation by key client staff members in leading roles). Naming these less pleasant features also helps you to compete with lower prices offered by rivals.

USE 'A LA CARTE' MENUS TO ENCOURAGE CLIENTS TO DEFINE WHAT IS VALUE FOR THEM

A third option to create the sense of price parity and reasonableness is to present the components of the solution initially as an 'à la carte' list (most expensive element first) and then configured into 'set meal' options. Here the price difference is that the configured meals offer better value, but the 'best value' (comparing individual item prices with set meal price) is the one you think is the best option for the client.

Each individual item has to be described in some detail (yours *is* a fancy restaurant) with the estimated benefits and any risks associated with them being taken in isolation. The costs of each element can also be presented as a range, to highlight the uncertainty of the price and encourage a debate with the customer about which aspects of the outcome/return they really value.

The 'set meals' highlight the overall benefits of complete solutions – both the 'hard' and 'soft' value of the outcomes. Again, these should be arranged from most to least expensive.

This approach plays on both transparency of costs and also the idea of price relationships (and trade-offs that are always made in assembling a solution). It works well if your company offers standard solutions but can also tailor solutions to deliver a more reliable or valuable result.

People prefer the sure thing to the gamble, but they would rather gamble than accept a sure loss, as Kahneman and Tversky established in their famous research, in which choices made were not entirely logical in economic terms.

Putting it all together

The comparisons clients make between different prices and different options can be used to focus them on the best option. This may be important not just in terms of sale price but also to build consensus between stakeholders who are resisting the idea of the purchase at all. The 'compromise' solution is often the second-highest price because 'downgrading' the expenditure indicates that the sponsor has listened and reduced the overall cost.

In presenting prices, you need to avoid the complaints many people have about the difficulty they have comparing the real costs of services like mobile-phone packages. Only 29 per cent of mobile-phone subscribers describe themselves as loyal. There are frequent complaints about price transparency, to the point where several stores and websites advise individual customers on the best deal for them. The inability to compare prices easily is irritating to B2B customers trying to choose between options and providers and many will insist that prices are presented in a way that enables them to do this.

The framing of gains and losses is easily manipulated by words in the working vocabulary of any salesperson (or con artist). In one study, a 'decrease in wages of 7 per cent in a company operating in a recession with substantial unemployment and zero inflation' was judged unfair by 65 per cent of people but the sentence 'only increasing wages by 5 per cent in an environment of recession with substantial unemployment and 12 per cent inflation' was seen as acceptable by 78 per cent of people surveyed. Even though the effect on their pay packet was identical, the form of words detracted from the idea of a sure loss.

9 TO PROCURE IS HUMAN...

'Cecil Graham: *What is a cynic?*
Lord Darlington: *A man who knows the price of everything
and the value of nothing.*
Cecil Graham: *And a sentimentalist, my dear Darlington, is a
man who sees an absurd value in everything and doesn't know
the market price of any single thing.*'
Oscar Wilde, Lady Windermere's Fan

Many people in sales demonize the procurement function. They
upset deals you thought were done, they seem to evaluate proposals
to a completely different set of rules, they treat the sales team in a
high-handed manner. Of course, we all want to avoid these demons,
perhaps because they remind us of our own less attractive qualities.

There are three common approaches to dealing with Procurement:

1. Marginalize them. Let your sponsor deal with their attempt to
   shave their target percentage off the final price.
2. Inflate the price to allow them to get their percentage and the
   sponsoring client to get the solution.
3. Try to make your service or solution a 'special case', beyond
   the reach of Procurement.

Any such tactic can work, depending on the nature of your
relationship with the sponsoring client. When the sponsor coaches
you about how to circumvent Procurement – for example, three
smaller projects rather than one large one, to bring the number
below Procurement's radar – this may work, especially if your
client is very senior and can break the rules or this is a non-
competitive bid. Many clients are irritated by Procurement's
power to upset and delay the decision to do a project, especially
when the budget has been allocated to them in the first place.

Successful salespeople are rather divided about the best way to
deal with Procurement, but generally they see the demonization
as a negative:

'Procurement has a role, not just in government work where they represent the first line of independent scrutiny of spending, which the public expects. As companies outsource and delegate more of their operations to outside companies – largely because technology allows them to do this – they want to reap the benefits of the economies of scale that those outsourcing companies provide. This is hard to evaluate, but necessary if the client is going to get a "fair" price. As solutions providers, we have to work with them and not see them as the enemy, because they have a legitimate role. I think of them as traffic wardens; nobody likes them, but without them congestion and parking access would be worse.'

From the perspective of the seller – and sometimes the sponsor – procurement people are not always the best at estimating the true value of a solution. They are usually accountants and trained to compare the price tags on the offers over deliverables to see whether your proposal offers good value for money. They like competitive bid situations. They get their power when the decision-makers are in a quandary. But in the end they can't actually decide which bid to support, because unless your solution relates to sourcing or procurement itself, in most organizations this isn't ultimately their final responsibility.

This is important to remember. As the seller, you are dealing with advisers and, like consultants, non-execs and even spouses, it is as well to deal fairly with anybody who is part of the decision-maker's risk-management tactics. Because of their role as arbitrators and auditors, procurement people tend to resist – or not be aware of – the salesperson's charm offensive. But in the end they have an interest in the company's future progress and their own interests as well, just like any other stakeholder.

INVOLVE THEM IN YOUR THINKING AND PREPARATION

Procurement functions vary widely in how far they are involved in different stages in the process. They may identify or shortlist potential suppliers, design the RFP process, communicate with bidders, negotiate, evaluate supplier performance, and so on, or they may stay out of the picture until the deal is nearly done. This is in part to ensure their impartiality and ability to analyse the proposals.

Given their various possible roles, it is important to understand from a potential prospect how and when the Procurement function will be involved, and discuss the process with them as you would with other stakeholder groups. If Procurement is coordinating the issue of the RFP, then this is easier than if the prospect wants to keep them in the dark until a draft proposal has been written. 'How to handle Procurement' is a topic that can crop up at any point, but it needs to be addressed directly with the prospect as soon as a proposal is being mooted.

FIND OUT ABOUT THEIR VIEWS, GOALS AND CONSTRAINTS

Because procurement people can be marginalized in their own company, you may find them more receptive than you imagine.

The guidelines for dealing with stakeholders apply: identify their perception of the issues, their vision for the future of this part of the business, their understanding about barriers and supporting factors in line with beneficial change, their part in the decision. Treating them as stakeholders in the company's success (and therefore the successful launch of a solution) is key, even if their department will not be directly affected.

There will be things they are not prepared to discuss, especially in competitive bid situations, as they will be aware that they might give one bidder some advantage, which could inhibit the objectivity of their contribution. But just as you are pleasant to the auditors and try to hide some of your resentment at the 'extra' work they give you, you should recognize that this is their job and be as cooperative as you can. This often makes things easier for the prospective sponsor as well.

USE PEOPLE WHO TALK THEIR LANGUAGE

Negotiating with Procurement comes later. Salespeople I spoke with had a wide range of experience, some saying that the real decision-makers liked to negotiate on behalf of the preferred bidders, others describing situations where the sponsors washed their hands of the whole negotiation process.

Several salespeople made the same point: salespeople aren't that good at talking about finance with accountants. 'Send the Finance Director to do any negotiating', they recommended, 'as he will speak the same language as Procurement.' As Procurement often use a version of cost–utility or cost–benefit analysis to compare options, it is as well to have somebody who can argue about method as well as result.

The net of the negotiation is a desire for a price reduction, even if your bid represented the best value. In this negotiation, it is important to be able to articulate the risk implications of any short cuts to your proposal. Short of showing your profit margins on the bid – which sometimes is the expectation – you may need to discuss with your Finance Director the 'walk away' number from either the risk or the profit perspective.

Putting it all together

When stakeholders or clients are difficult, the advice is usually 'Get closer', even though your tendency is to do the opposite to avoid the grief. Procurement are not the enemy; they are part of the purchasing process for many organizations, set up to advise and organize, but rarely to ultimately decide.

Treating them as stakeholders, people with a legitimate interest, seems to produce the best result.

10 REQUESTS FOR PROPOSAL (RFPs) ARE HONEYPOTS

'Speak truth to power.'
Quaker pamphlet

Most salespeople, and many clients, hate RFPs. Even clients admit that they probably don't stimulate the most creative proposals. Clients use RFPs for various reasons:

- To create a 'level playing field', with no advantage to any potential bidder. This is the equivalent of the job advert, but for a service or solution need.
- Because they have to show that they haven't been influenced unduly by personal factors in awarding the contract. Some potential auditor conducting a due diligence can see that procurement guidelines have been followed. This is about both fairness and the need for the client to cover themselves.
- When they believe they can self-diagnose their requirements enough to brief you, the supplier, about what they need. This is true for a commodity purchase – clients know how much steel they want to buy and all its features, so they just want to get the best supplier with the best price – but is usually only partly true for more professional services and complex solutions, even if the person writing the RFP left your company the day before to join the customer.
- When the purchase is perceived to be risky due to its size, cost or complexity. The client can get the bidders to educate them about the risks at no cost.

RFPs can increase the cost of selling and buying. I have known consortia rack up over £1 million in cost of sales for complex government bids. This investment has to be reflected in the price which the customer tries to recoup through negotiation, adding further to the cost. Put like that, it's a bit depressing. Compared to an open dialogue with your clients, RFPs *are* depressing, which is why anybody who likes selling is not motivated by the RFP unless they can bend those rules to provide a better, more interesting answer...

Many companies respond to RFPs only if the size of the contract makes it worth their while. Why do *you* respond?

Providers respond to RFPs:

• **in markets where they are the norm**

This means large governmental contracts, which might otherwise be open to bribery or some other sort of abuse, but can also mean any large sourcing or procurement deal in a major company. If you want to operate in these markets, you know you will have to engineer out the cost of bidding, so that when it is your 'turn' to be shortlisted you have registered your interest.

• **when they need the work**

In many economies, when recession strikes – or VUCA (volatility, uncertainty, complexity and ambiguity) seems to be the norm (which, nowadays, it is in many places) – government spending has traditionally been the way to keep the economy going; infrastructure projects of all sorts will be launched with RFPs. So if you are a service or solution provider, you may be forced to bid or lay people off.

• **because they want to enter a market that buys by RFP.**

Some companies cut their teeth on the process by bidding for contracts, which they aren't that interested in, because they would like to work for this customer in other areas. There is a sort of myth that if you bid often the client takes your interest seriously, as if bidding builds up a sense of client obligation, and in the end you will be shortlisted.

But salespeople should be sceptical. As one experienced salesperson told me:

> 'The head of the department rang regarding the RFP they had sent out. He said "It's definitely you, but you have to pitch it." I know him well. So I said: "Thank you for your confidence. But are you also saying that, if in future I *don't* get a call like this, I shouldn't answer your RFPs?" There was a bit of a silence. Presumably they just ring up the preferred supplier every time...'

LOOK CAREFULLY AT THE ACCESS THE RFP PROCESS GIVES YOU TO DECISION-MAKERS

The process of creating an RFP is illuminating. RFPs are often written by gatekeepers keen to impress their masters. They are often a compromise between the different, most important stakeholders, who only want to rehearse their differences when it comes to the beauty parade of shortlisted finalists; in fact, they can decide not to go ahead at all at this point. Occasionally, they are written by people who have a vested interest in one aspect of the project (maybe incumbent consultants who are working with the client already). Sometimes they are a cosmetic process and the client just wants some other providers to quote prices against which they will negotiate with the preferred provider (who may already be working with them). RFP intentions are tricky to unravel.

Most RFPs spell out the decision-making process. For example:

1. All interested parties submit an information pack setting out their qualification to bid.
2. Invitations to bid are issued to the lucky parties who have passed this preliminary test. These people sign an agreement.
3. The bidders receive more details on the need.
4. The bidders are allowed one hour with a panel to ask questions before submitting draft bids.
5. A review panel looks at all the bids.

If you get access to decision-makers, here are some key questions to ask:

- Who is/are the sponsor(s) of this project? Ask this from the point of view of who will be providing the budget and also from the perspective of who decides on where to award the project.
- What are the criteria for making the decision? Ask about soft criteria such as 'cultural fit', as well as hard ones such as budget.
- What happens if the sponsors involved disagree about the best supplier?
- What happens if we, as potential suppliers, withdraw? This last question is about being excluded from future opportunities, if the process seems inequitable or too expensive for your company.

LOOK EVEN MORE CAREFULLY AT THE ACCESS THE RFP PROCESS GIVES YOU TO END-USERS

The designation of needs depends on where you sit. Senior managers believe they understand the issues in the front line, but users often have a different view. You need to speak to those most affected by the solution you propose as well as to the sponsors.

If you cannot do this and rely entirely on the words of senior managers to spell out the solution to the (senior managers') needs, you put a number of things at risk:

- There may be a later rejection of your solution even if the senior clients agree.
- Your proposed solution may not actually deliver.
- The service might meet all the agreed criteria in terms of performance and outcomes achieved, but you may have created 300 unhappy people lower down the company who will not hesitate to shout abuse to anybody who will listen.

You need access to only a small but representative sample of the people whose lives will be affected and whose behaviour your solution will influence. If you do get access, key questions are:

1. What does success look like to you?
2. What factors will help us achieve or hinder us from achieving this with you?
3. How do you feel about the company changing things in this way?
4. If you were drafting the RFP, what metric(s) of performance would you include?
5. If you were choosing the supplier, what selection criteria would you use?

CONSIDER THE IMPLICATIONS OF NO-BID OPTIONS

The salesperson frowned. I had asked the question, 'How do you deal with companies that won't budge from the "zero access" stipulation in an RFP?' (This is quite common in services which the client decides are 'just technical', like doing a due diligence on a potential acquisition.)

He replied, 'I say, "You won't get the best proposal if we can't discuss ideas with you and your colleagues."'

'And if they still won't budge?'

'We won't bid. They are going to be hellish as clients.'

Walking away from a potential sale is a powerful tactic and must be used with care. It indicates that you do not want the business (obviously), but it is also communicating that you do not want to help or provide a service to the customer. It is this emotional component to not bidding which makes the matter so sensitive; having positioned yourself as the client's service partner, to walk off the pitch is giving them a slap in the face. You will dress up your decision in a number of ways – bad timing; we don't really have exactly the right resources for this; we have just won another big contract in the same area with a competitor and there are ethical aspects – but, no matter how you represent your wish to step back, it is a rejection of the client.

Consider a conditional withdrawal from the sale. Ask yourself under what circumstances you would continue to bid. If these circumstances are something the client should consider, then make them your conditions. Some clients have to issue RFPs for purchases of any kind over a certain value. Indicating your company policy might influence their process if you are a market leader. But they must not be changes to win some advantage over the competition. You have to demonstrate how it is in the client's interest, too.

Putting it all together

RFPs help the client to organize competitive bids. They purport to provide a level playing field for competition, but rely on clients who can accurately self-diagnose what they need. For commodities this specification is likely to be accurate, for solutions and professional services less so. 'The RFP reduces every purchase to the level of a commodity, unless the client is sophisticated.'

To bid well, you must understand the context and impact of your proposed solution. This means access to decision-makers and 'users' – people in the front line who will have to change as a result. If these are denied, you enter a lottery where previous suppliers will have an advantage and you might consider withdrawing. If you do, consider the message you are giving your client.

11 CLOSING TAKES PATIENCE

'Persistence pays, says conventional sales thinking. Persistence in pursuing bad business wastes valuable resources, says diagnostic sales thinking.'
Jeff Thull

Product salespeople have an axiom: 'Close early, close often.' It is a way of showing the customer that it's time to make a decision. Buying a car? 'What will it take from me to have you sign today?' asks the salesman at the earliest opportunity. As customers, our idle speculation about a purchase just got real...

B2B contracts may need a different approach. Most salespeople use the idea of the proposal to accelerate the client's thinking and decision-making. They start sending the client the different parts as soon as they can... drip, drip. Agree the background to the bid, the context, which is driving the idea of change or the need for the service. Drip. Define the desirable outcomes. Specify the solution that produces these outcomes and the evidence to substantiate that your solution does this. Drip, drip. Elaborate on the options, if necessary. Quote a price and payment and delivery schedule. Drip. Bucket full. Suddenly, the client has an offer on the table to consider.

Often, clients will start by asking the price, because there are no tickets on solutions. This isn't a close by them, just an information gap. How much might I need in my budget?

'When a client asks any question, you have to answer, even when you have no idea what the final answer will be. Otherwise you look evasive. One tricky question – often at the first meeting – is "How much?" At this point there is no agreement about scope at all, and you have no idea of their budget, so you really have no clue what the price to them is going to be. I answer in terms of other installations or projects. After describing the scope and the value of the outcomes, I always say, "For that our client paid x…", not "We charged x…". I start with a big-ticket case and then move to a smaller one. You don't want to lose the opportunity to anchor their thinking about price point. If they wince, then I got it about right. If they show no emotion at the first price, I pitched it too low.'

Quoting a price is often the first step to closing a deal, but timing is critical.

SELL SMALL, BUT THINK BIG FOR FIRST-TIME BUYERS

With new clients, don't try to sell a big contract all at once. First-time buyers are often testing the water, so a chance for you to work with them and show them what you can do makes sense on both sides. It is a test of their willingness to pay as well as the value of your people, your company and your solutions.

These up-front projects are called many things – feasibility studies, specification projects, gap analyses – but in practice they all come down to the same thing: a paid proposal with some insight for the client. They should be scoped so that the prospect you are talking with can approve the budget without further consultation. Then you can close straight away.

This is your metaphorical foot in the door, and it may give you some advantages over competitors, although this is not guaranteed. Clients sometimes allow different companies access to test out whether they are just seeking to make the case for their solution or whether they are using the project to genuinely consider what would work best for the client.

'I had a client who really put us through the wringer on the proposal. We wrote three completely different ones, but eventually we won. Afterwards, I asked him why he made us – and other companies – do all that work. "I didn't know what solution I wanted," he said. "Each solution presented showed me that what I had briefed everybody on was what I didn't want."'

But closing early on a small project makes sense, nonetheless (unless you need to land a big one soon, because you'll be paid a bonus or to save the company).

WIN THE RACE BY STARTING WORK

When there is a bid process with competitors, most vendors wait until the last minute to submit their proposals. This is partly for internal reasons – a large bid will be subject to scrutiny by many internal stakeholders in your company – but also because clients may reveal more information later in the process, after being subjected to pressure from you or other bidders (as long as they subscribe to the general government rule about transparency with all bidders about all questions and answers to the RFP document). There is no particular advantage in delivering early under such circumstances.

Where the situation is less structured and may not be competitive, then moving to 'working with', rather than selling, is critical. This means that the team might start work before the final contracts are agreed, on the verbal agreement that 'things will be sorted out later'. This is 'closing' to prevent the process becoming a formal competitive bid process, or other companies getting wind of what your client is starting to think.

One consulting firm I know does this regularly, starting work on the project before exact terms of reference are established, on the basis of trust. To do this, they need to establish that a delay would mean an unnecessary risk to the client, which is usually not that difficult. From the client's point of view there is no contract, so his company is not taking much risk in letting the consultants start work. The consulting firm lets this run for a couple of weeks and then sends an invoice as an 'upfront payment for expenses' to test their client's authority to pay. It sounds risky, but they claim it keeps out competition and rarely creates problems: 'If you trust your clients, you support them, even if they don't have the funds to pay you right now' – or so their reasoning runs.

Starting work is a pre-emptive close. It is a better competitive tactic than getting closure on the fine details of the bid, as you are by definition 'ahead', in both knowledge of the client's need and the development of the solution. For this reason, separating agreement on the scope of work from negotiation on the costs and payment terms can sometimes also make sense (unless you know that you have over-scoped the project in terms of the client's budget). Negotiations over price can be protracted and can affect the date when the sale can be attributed, so it can help to offer a small discount for an early agreement on the price, if the attribution date is important to you or your business. All proposals should have some caveat like 'Prices quoted are good for the next 30 days'.

CLOSE TOO EARLY AND MISS OUT ON SCOPE EXPANSION; CLOSE TOO LATE AND WATCH YOUR COST OF SALES SOAR

There is a tension between the desire to get the job finalized and the final size of the job. As more stakeholders become involved, the scope of work tends to expand to accommodate their interests and needs. How far this happens depends on the sponsor's control over the stakeholders and how far she wants to 'keep them in the tent'. Some sales roll on and on, gathering moss, and then are settled in an instant. Others lose focus and are sometimes abandoned altogether. Deciding on when to invoke the need to close is a fine judgement by the sales team.

One way to do this – again favoured by consultants – is to threaten to send your clients a bill. As the debates continue, the continuing cost of sales racks up – as does the cost of buying – and the choice of 'pay something or we stop working on this' can focus the client's mind. This probably works only when your organization calculates that the cost of sales will not be covered by the margin you expect on the job, so the concern is real; you might really need to cut your losses and withdraw.

Putting it all together

Although 'closing' is generally a test of a good product salesperson, with B2B services and solutions the complexity of both the decision on scope and the politics of the decision-making mean that the client often needs time to come to a conclusion. It may well be a case of 'hanging on in there'.

Doing something chargeable for your client, however small, effectively closes the business. Everything else is now an extension. But doing this without a contract can be risky with clients you do not know well. They, too, may prefer the certainty of a smaller paid study to check out your company's qualities.

12 THE 'WALK AWAY' POINT DETERMINES YOUR TACTICS

'We cannot negotiate with people who say what's mine is mine and what's yours is negotiable.'
John Kennedy

The aim of negotiation is agreement, on price or scope or timing or staffing, or any combination of these factors. There are excellent books on negotiation but the overall impression created from talking with good salespeople is that they would say 'Don't negotiate' – at least not as an afterthought to a decision about scope that has been agreed.

'"We like your bid and we would like to offer you the contract," they say. Then there's a little pause. "Subject to negotiation." I want to say, "What do you think we have been doing all these weeks with our adjustments and our service-level agreements and proposals? Having a jolly picnic?" Our cost of sales is through the roof – and so is their cost of buying, but they don't think like that. They think they have got you and you have gone so far that you won't turn back for 10 per cent less.'

'It was Christmas Eve and the office party was taking place that day. We had an outstanding bid for a £10 million computer-assisted design system and the guy from Procurement calls me up and asks me to come down to their office because he wants to sign. It's a three-hour drive and I will miss the party, but we have been working hard on this client, so I go. I'm kept waiting in Reception for over an hour, then he appears, full of apologies: "I didn't know you'd arrived." I bet. Then he gets out the paperwork and says "Before I sign, I need two things; a further 20 per cent discount and..." He lists other elements in the contract which we had discussed but which they weren't prepared to pay for. I'm furious. "Look. It's Christmas Eve and I won't get home until late. I have missed the annual party. All because you said you were going to sign." His face registers nothing. "I'm going to have to borrow your phone." I really *am* furious. He looks a bit shamefaced. "It's over there. What do you want it for?" Without thinking, I say, "I'm going to call your Director of Design and tell him that, after all this, after all these discussions, after all these weeks, he isn't going to get his system on 1 January as we had promised." I start to walk over to the phone, which is in the room next door. He shouts, "It's OK. Look, I've signed. I just thought I ought to see if there was any more juice in the orange." A pause. "Happy Christmas!" What a nerve. You have to be prepared to walk away. When the value is there, you have to be prepared to leave it all on the table.'

To avoid these situations, you need to be tough with your client's organization – because frequently it is not the presenting sponsor who is negotiating but some other function, like Procurement, which has a target to meet to reduce costs.

KNOW THE VALUE OF THE BID YOU MAKE

Solutions are designed to create value for clients. In designing a solution, you have to understand the client's current process and where the current costs and risks lie. Assuming the client has given you access to their current system or accurate data about the current state of affairs, you will be able to assess the potential gains and then decide whether or not to bid. (If you can't see a way to create value, you probably won't bid.)

Architecting the deal means you try to maximize the value to them and to your own business, but this means knowing what improvement you can promise the client at what price. Commercial value to most clients is the difference between the current performance return at a known cost and the new performance at a promised cost. This value is what should be reflected in the final price you quote. So, if you transform their current performance at £1 million with an annual cost of £0.5 million to a future performance of £2 million at the same price, the value you propose is a net increase of £1 million. If you know that for them to deliver the same number would require them to double their costs, then you are also saving them £0.5 million. So you propose an annual charge of £0.5 million.

To negotiate with Procurement usually requires you to be able to define the risks involved for the client of spending less than £0.5 million to produce this result. This makes Procurement think more broadly about the value and discuss these risks with your sponsor. Sometimes they leave the price alone but suggest something like a risk–reward payment process instead.

The key is to know what the real value of your offer is to the client and that your prices and profit margins are in line with the market. If you are cleverer than the competition at managing your costs, this is not a subject for negotiation. By definition, clients will expect you to be more efficient than them.

BE PREPARED TO WALK

Here's a recent conversation with Procurement in the US, who rang me up about a long-standing training and development relationship I have had with a client – their European operation:

"'Hi, this is Bob in Procurement. We would like to talk about reducing your prices to us. You have worked with us for… seven years?"

"Correct. It's been a very interesting and enjoyable relationship. Reflected in the fact that during that time I haven't put up our prices at all for anything I have done for you."

"OK. This conversation is about reducing our costs. So what sort of discount could you consider offering us?"

"I already did, in effect. My prices haven't reflected inflation at all over seven years."

"No, I mean in the future. You run courses for us, right?"

"Not as many as I used to. Last year I ran two and the previous year four, which was the usual rate."

"So, if we offered you more courses, how much of a discount would you offer us?"

"I don't think there is demand at the moment in Europe for more courses, otherwise I *would* be doing four, not two."

"But if we could..."

"Certainly, I'd consider it. Would you pay travel time to Asia to compensate me?"

"No, no, we are talking about reducing your cost to us."

"Well, why would I do that? Take on more work at a lower margin?"

"Because you are an important supplier to us."

"Don't you mean, because you are an important client of mine? Which you are. I'm very happy to do this work. Look, Bob. You have a job to do. My job is designing and delivering courses, which are worth every penny of what I charge, in my view – and in the view of others, or I wouldn't still be working here after seven years. Students deliver sales as a result well in excess of any fees I have charged... I make good money doing this, but so does your business. Why would I discount?"'

I didn't especially want to win the argument, but when Bob realizes that his offer – increased volume – doesn't equate to reduced price, there's nothing he can do. He doesn't really control the allocation of consultants to work. He knows only that I am a bit more expensive than other consultants they use. Because I will walk, he has to talk to the sponsors and ask them what to do. (Interestingly, this was a turning point for me in my relationship with the company. The sponsors were embarrassed – and they need not have been.)

SAY HOW YOU WILL HANDLE POST-AGREEMENT NEGOTIATIONS, IF AT ALL

In any service business, there is a direct relationship between cost and scope of work – services businesses are time-based – so, if you alter the price paid, then either the service provider has to reduce their margin or the scope of what is provided has to change. In service businesses, cost of sales can be seen as 'lost production time'. Both parties know this, which is why daily rates for specialists are often part of the scoping discussions with sponsors. What sponsors don't know – and providers sometimes do not either – is exactly how long (cost) things will take to deliver. This may be because the technology is new, there is a risky critical path or because the estimates for client and other consortium members' contributions are hard to make.

This is why solutions providers factor dealing with these risks into either their margins or the total budget and time for the job. The more strategic and leading-edge a project or solution, the bigger the risks tend to be for the provider. The project manager is key in managing this process within the budget, which is why all providers want their own project managers in charge. Everybody wants to do a good job for the client, but they have to help the provider manage risks in this way.

Clients don't necessarily understand this thinking. They are worried that the experts are pulling a fast one and making simple things more complex to inflate the price. They think that they should be able to negotiate on price independent of the solution delivered. In effect, it is as if they were buying a product where the development costs are sunk costs.

Some salespeople refuse retrospectively to negotiate on price without negotiating on scope (effort, time, quality or number of deliverables, performance of solution). This seems fair, but you have to be prepared to walk. You also have to say upfront that this is your company's policy. There is no point in making a client fall for your solution and then surprise them by making a stand against their attempt to negotiate.

Fair negotiation is based on the value of the outcomes you deliver to your client. So you need to know about current costs and risks and outcomes first, and then consider the gains they will make in terms of better returns or reduced costs and risks (or both). When you know the commercial value to them, you can decide on a fair price.

But once you have established this – and shared it with the client – you have to be prepared to stand firm and potentially leave the deal on the table.

13 REFERRALS, NOT FERAL SALESPEOPLE

'Our social ties influence our satisfaction with life, our cognitive skills and how resistant we are to infections and chronic disease.'

Susan Pinker

The theory that we are only six relationship steps from anybody we want to meet is, of course, an approximation. But social media increase the chances that we are quite closely 'related' to far more people than we realize. Although you target people based on their potential as a buyer for your service or solution, good salespeople know that it is much easier to get a meeting through a mutual relationship than a cold call. Research shows that 70 per cent of satisfied service clients are prepared to refer people to others, but only 30 per cent of service providers ask. Finding links cuts short the alternative: long hours of cold approaches, spam mail, cold-calling and other direct-marketing methods.

LinkedIn is brilliant for helping you think about this. If you are assiduous about getting and accepting introductions, you can check whether there are any connections between your existing contacts and the target client. Obviously, always respond positively to anybody who wants to connect with you, as you never know exactly when their contact list might be useful. At the same time, prioritize contacts that are suitably senior; senior people tend to have more contacts. Using LinkedIn or other social media also reinforces the principle that 'people buy from people' and your company works on this principle of the personal contract.

Furthermore

According to evolutionary psychologist Robin Dunbar, 150 is the maximum number of meaningful relationships that the human brain can manage. Studies in the UK and the Netherlands showed that people varied in the amount of face-to-face time they needed to really stay friends; anything from 18 months to seven years. Without face-to-face contact, social relationships get replaced with other 'friends'.

A bit of lateral thinking reveals many other sources of introduction, often closer to hand. Professionals – lawyers, accountants, bankers, consultants – and sometimes other salespeople are all looking to improve their business development capability and reciprocal introductions are part of this. Have you thought of using your company's advisers to help you in this way? Your suppliers may also be able to help with introductions. Generally, well-networked people of all sorts make the best introducers; they enjoy seeing other relationships flourish and being the broker.

It is also worth exploring what relationships exist within your own company; salespeople tend to be a bit protective of their contacts, like journalists with their sources, but most of the rest of your company may well be open to making an introduction; group emails and voicemails can often throw up names and ideas for points of entry. A family contact, a sports club friend, the person who has the allotment next door... Ironically, because salespeople tend to see themselves as on the road, they can neglect their relationships with people in their own company who may be the stepping stone to client relationships they want. Often, people know people who have left, who now work in the same industry as your target client, and who can help. People are often generous with their contacts, as long as they trust the intermediary.

As trade is reciprocal, it is important to help others in this way – perhaps with access to your company's managers. As Robert Cialdini and others have observed, a sense of obligation is a powerful way to influence others and it is not proportional to the 'value' of the original favour, as long as that favour was

spontaneous and not manipulative. Many of the salespeople
I interviewed do not see social or family relationships as any
different from those through which they generate business.
The family business is still the model for more than half of all
businesses in Europe, so this is perhaps less surprising than it
first appears.

ANALYSE YOUR NETWORK MAP – WHO KNOWS WHO? WHO KNOWS YOU?

When planning how best to structure your campaign, you need
a map to help you identify the lie of the land and the position
of enemy forces (if any). The lie of the land in a company is best
understood with an organization chart, which is the first step
to identifying whom you might need to meet as sponsors and
stakeholders in the solution. An inside contact may help you
with who holds what budget and who has responsibility for
which aspects of the strategy. They can also help you to identify
competitors and incumbent suppliers. Often, the longer-term
play – making contacts with several insiders a couple of removes
from the actual decision-makers – works best.

Insiders also help you understand how decisions are made – who
has the power to decide what, who influences whom, particularly
if your success is of benefit to them. Decision-making authority
is rarely as simple as the organization chart might indicate; some
managers think that after consultation their task, as the boss, is
to decide. Others believe that consensus must be reached before
a major decision is taken. Others again believe this is simply
too slow and that they are paid to make the decision and then
persuade others to agree.

Although such preferences may be cultural as much as individual,
it is a very useful to know how, in the past, larger B2B decisions
have been made. It is also interesting to know whether there
was much criticism or resistance to the implementation of
previous choices. Your informants can also tell you about who
else is sniffing around. Information about competitor activity in
targeted organizations can either come from your own network –

most of you will know people who work for rival firms – or from inside. What is being discussed with which competitor is a good way of checking whether your initial analysis of the priorities is correct. You may be able to leapfrog the process by suggesting your own company as a potential bidder for the work under consideration.

GET AN INTRODUCTION TO THE PERSON YOU THINK MIGHT BE INTERESTED

People who know you will often make introductions without your having to tell them in great detail what your company's interest is. Successful salespeople are honest about their intentions. Senior professionals involved in selling professional services often find being direct about selling rather tricky. With the image of the second-hand car dealership firmly embedded in their imagination, they think that being a salesperson somehow contradicts the idea of being a trusted adviser – a lawyer or an accountant.

This is nonsense. I once coached a technically brilliant junior partner in a professional services firm to become their top salesperson simply by advising him – when meeting new potential clients – to say, 'We'd like to find a way to do business with you.' He had very sophisticated social skills but found the idea of selling uncomfortable, so would meet clients over and over again, giving them loads of value but never asking for the business.

COMPLETE THE LOOP BY RECIPROCATING WITH SOMETHING OF VALUE

Astonishingly few people remember to thank their intermediary for the introduction, even when this leads eventually to a large deal. The first rule of networking is 'create goodwill', and if your contact was part of that big sale then you just withdrew from that goodwill account and need to make a deposit. What you do will depend on the individual, but boxes of chocolates, bunches of flowers or champagne may be less appropriate than reciprocal introductions – perhaps fixing up a meeting with somebody who can help the intermediary's career, or providing one of their children with a summer job. For the same reason, it is also important to continue to recognize the value of the introduction by keeping the intermediary informed – in a way that honours client discretion – about the progress of the sale, perhaps giving them some information about your company in the process.

If this introduction is successful, then you will want to ask again. Social media networkers, those with the most 'friends', are rarely the most sociable in person. They may even prefer the shop window of friendship to real hugs. Good intermediaries are people who physically network, too, because the bandwidth of the drink after work or the lunch is far broader than Facebook. When introductions don't work, it is often that the introducer's relationship with your target is far weaker than they imagine it to be; they think they know the person well enough to give you access, but in reality they cannot.

The other reason to reinforce the goodwill with the intermediary who made the introduction is that we know solutions clients considering their options will at some point actively evaluate not just the solution but also the provider. It is therefore highly likely that your target – now become a prospect – will revert to the intermediary who made the introduction in the first place. What would you like this person to say at this point? 'He's a friend of mine from the golf club. I don't know anything about his company', or something more considered? Although this person is not necessarily a stakeholder in the solution or the sale itself, their involvement may turn out to be just as crucial to the decision-making process as somebody closer to the action.

Putting it all together

Getting to your targeted client is often a knight's move – sideways as well as forwards. It mostly involves introductions from others in your network, preferably those you have kept well informed about what you sell and who know you well in a social as well as professional capacity. For the intermediary, the only risk of making the introduction is if you fail to perform and they have therefore wasted their contact's (your target's) time.

Having something concrete and valuable to discuss helps to secure the introduction: research or analysis that is relevant to an issue or the client's industry. Insight can be controversial and this may help the conversation.

People often fail to cast the net widely enough in their search for access. Your own company can often help. Your personal network may also be able to assist if you allow them to. Social media may also help, but it is usually the good face-to-face networkers who do this best; they believe in the power of the lunch and the handshake and they are more likely therefore to help you to get to either.

14 A 'STRATEGIC' SOLUTION IS WORTH MORE

'Sales isn't about getting people to buy from you. Sales is about finding out what problems people have, and offering them solutions.'

Jarod Kintz

The most valuable outcomes are often those that align with your client's strategies. Commodity solutions are heat-seeking missiles, homing in on the warmest targets, but the really valuable solutions change your clients' thinking about their future. The salesperson not only changes the way the client does business, but they also educate the client about new possibilities for the ways to do business.

Finding this alignment requires a change in the way you, as a salesperson, think and behave, too. You have to understand what is happening for your clients and *their* customers in *their* markets, not just look for the sweet-spot opportunity. The main components of strategic thinking are not that complicated; how a business creates and captures value is constantly influenced by changes in its environment. These trends can be beneficial or threatening. Strategies are decisions about where to act and invest to grow the business, given these environmental challenges and opportunities – for example a new entrant muscling in on your client's 'space' in that market. But the environment is constantly changing and these changes create pressures on senior managers to find new solutions.

ANTICIPATE WHAT IS CAUSING THE PRESSURE ON THEIR BUSINESS MODEL

Strategic thinking about your client starts by considering what is happening in *their* markets and to *their* customers. There are always social trends and political or regulatory changes, as well as new technologies and economic forces at play, which affect how an organization makes money and competes. Many professional services firms rely on environmental changes to provide the client motivation for hiring them: privatization, nationalization, regulation of monopolies, changes in the law. As a client, if you read the environment wrong – as Kodak did the digital revolution in photography – you lose your shirt. Read it right and you could get the edge on a whole industry – viz. Apple and iTunes.

Senior people, who determine what gets invested where, are always thinking about this: how to stay ahead or, sometimes, how to survive. They are aware that their knowledge is often rather out of date, so the idea of educating a client to new ways of doing business is not so far-fetched. They want to know, even if they don't want to buy immediately.

But, before you educate, you have to do your homework on what issues they are facing in the market and consider how what you offer – solutions, products or services – helps them to perform better in this ever-changing environment. You need to find the answers to these questions:

- Who are their competitors?
- How is this client's business differentiating itself?
- On what basis have they historically competed for customers and trade in this market?
- Is this enough for the future?
- What do they lack in terms of an ability to compete for customers?
- Who is responsible for sorting this out?
- What are the pressures on this person to deliver solutions to these issues?

Take a solution like leadership training. Leadership has become a hotter topic than management because of the increasing volatility and uncertainty in the business environment for almost all sectors. Where management is about stability, leadership is about change and creating a future. As a solution, leadership training offers an increased capacity for individual managers to cope with ambiguity productively, and in a way that excites their teams to better performance. It might even help the company to compete better if they have superior leaders: more agile, more strategic, more inspiring. Who has to sort this?

Usually the HR Director takes charge of this aspect of 'future-proofing' the management of the company, increasing their potential not just to find answers to market issues, but also to take people with them along a new strategic road. But to sell leadership development you will need to understand the sorts of pressures on the business and then relate these to the outcomes your solution provides – for example improved retention of talent or greater potential at the individual level to cope and capitalize on a VUCA (volatile, uncertain, complex, ambiguous) world.

CONSIDER WHAT THE OUTCOMES WILL MEAN FOR THE CLIENT AND THEIR PERCEIVED VALUE

When you have discovered that the main trends for the industry are, say, technological and regulatory and that the market divides into low-cost/high-volume producers and high-cost/low-volume players... what next?

Think about what your solution delivers – or could deliver, with a little tweaking. Which of the outcomes it produces link to the priorities that many companies in this industry are likely to be considering? Some basic competitor analysis helps you decide which of its benefits or outcomes are likely to be received most positively – is it efficiency, effectiveness or risk reduction? When you know an industry well, you may be able to put a figure on what that outcome could be worth.

For example, pharmaceutical companies can have a bad time when drugs come off patent, as within 12 months they tend to lose a large percentage of their market share to generic competitors that can undercut their prices in the market. This is particularly critical if the drug is a blockbuster ($1 billion per year sales), as these sorts of losses will affect the share price. If your solution could transform, say, a 70 per cent loss of market share to only a 50 per cent loss of market share, you can work out what your solution is worth to the company.

All industries have repeating problems like this. For some, it might be an inefficient supply chain or managing inventory, or sluggish cost recovery. All industries try to innovate to resolve these longer-term issues, but innovation itself creates pressures, which raise the value of solutions, which mitigate risks.

Furthermore

Digital and social media are the latest challenge for many: projecting your brand to a highly sophisticated global audience, using the data from a wide range of sources and platforms to gain competitive advantage. If your solution can help your client to manage the pressures that this trend is creating, people will be interested in hearing what you have to say.

WORK OUT HOW BEST TO USE THIS INSIGHT AND KNOWLEDGE

An insight into the future is valuable to a client in its own right, irrespective of whether they then buy your solution. Once you are talking about the future, alternative strategies, competition, distinguishing competencies and the like, you are changing the way you serve clients. This is a long game – one that may take you in a very different direction from classic sales campaigns.

Insight is often about a different way of looking at something which the client is familiar with. Familiarity may blind people to alternative ways of seeing something and therefore they find problems harder to solve or opportunities remain invisible. A genuine insight opens the door to new possibilities for the person receiving it; the problem is less complex, the opportunity is riskier but more valuable. An insight is inspirational – the shock of the new or maybe an epiphany. The client has been trapped in a habitual way of thinking about their situation or company and you have unlocked the door.

See Chapter 6 for some ways to encourage the client to reframe the problem.

It's risky, of course, telling your client that their perspective on the situation is partial or flawed. Initially, you might be well advised to be circumspect in your insights. Outsiders are useful if their analysis opens the client's eyes. But it is easy to get it wrong in quite a fundamental way without realizing it. The best positioning is often 'our hypothesis', or perhaps 'some intriguing findings'. This works when you explain that you have been thinking about your *own* strategy as a provider of solutions, and have therefore been looking at what is happening in *your* markets to *your* customers.

A blazing opportunity that your client might potentially overlook is always a good hook for a face-to-face meeting. Getting your problem analysis incorrect will not help the relationship; alerting your client to an opportunity 'which you are probably already considering' might work better. Even if your opportunity turns out not to be that big, you have demonstrated that you want to understand their business in a fundamental way.

Putting it all together

One thing that has an impact on a client's perception of the value of a solution is how it creates competitive advantage for them in their continuing struggle to stay ahead in their markets. Identify ways in which what your company offers can produce outcomes that will help the client to gain competitive advantage. Tell this to them in terms of maximizing opportunities (in the first place) and you may find it easier to get an initial meeting and also to demonstrate that you want to build a longer-term business relationship between your companies.

Even if this initial investment of time before making contact fails to deliver a meeting, you will find that the analysis and research pays off at some future point when you quote a statistic with authority or raise an issue when talking with another client, which demonstrates your understanding of the market.

15 OUTCOMES, NOT FEATURES

'Don't sell life insurance. Sell what life insurance can do.'
Ben Feldman

Great salespeople are not content to just memorize the features and benefits of the new solutions, arrange them into scripts and talk their way to victory. In the world where outcomes are valued, the features of your product or solution are profoundly dull to most of your customers. (Not all: there will still be specialists and geeks who love to trade technical details.) For most, it will be the beneficial changes your solution provides that customers are more interested in.

The kind of knowledge you offer includes insights about change, the impact of your solution on clients (and their customers) and clarity about what excites you personally about what you sell. Do you have personal experience of your solution and its impact? In a world where you are selling promises, you need to make sure they are authentic ones and ones that you personally find exciting.

KNOW HOW THE SOLUTION WORKS

Of course, you know what it does, but do you know *how* it does it? Mastery of the detail of the solution and its options is the baseline of all other knowledge, but it is only valuable to a client when it is adapted to their level of knowledge or interest. Anything else is boring, or confusing. Depending on your personal background – technical, managerial, professional – you will probably be more/less comfortable describing the solution to different audiences, but being able to communicate and answer detailed questions from a range of stakeholders is important for your personal credibility and that of your solution.

'I get myself tested by technicians, line managers and professionals in my own company before I meet clients. A briefing or a guide is rarely enough to ensure a more-than-competent performance in front of whoever else the client decides to bring to the meeting.'

Know about installation, and what the problems have been installing the solution in companies. Admitting that your company has learned how to avoid technical and other risks over time is reassuring to clients who will have had their own experiences of change led by technology or professionals.

BE ABLE TO DESCRIBE THE SOLUTION'S IMPACT

With the exception of untried solutions, you need to know what the impact of your proposed solution has been on client organizations who have bought it before.

There are two aspects to impact:

- The commercial and other benefits of this change
- What changed in the organization (and how the change was introduced)

The first aspect of impact requires you to have tracked the benefits of the solution over time, preferably in ways that relate to what the new client values. Tracking benefits is not easy unless you collect some baseline data at the start of the process against which you can compare the 'before' and 'after'. To make an effective prediction about the future impact on another business, you need to demonstrate that the drivers of these changes are constant between the two companies.

'Taking into account the underlying growth rate in GDP, in real terms our client achieved a 10 per cent growth rate in leads and a 8 per cent growth rate in sales closed in Europe. The growth rate for GDP is still the same, so you should be able to achieve similar results. What would that translate into in terms of revenue uplift, I wonder?'

Generally, customers assess business value in three ways: increasing revenues, lowered costs and reduced risks. This suggests that you should track the benefits of your solutions in terms of:

- quantitative results – performance improvements, revenue increases, efficiency gains
- qualitative results – impact on staff, customers, reduction in short-term risks
- strategic benefits – improved competitive positioning, better use of core assets, reduction of longer-term risks.

The second is relatively simple to describe in factual terms: the project plan, the best way to control implementation, your excellence in change management. If clients understand the benefit, they may need reassurance that the disruption will be worth the cost. So you need to know about how the solution affected stakeholders. Clients like to know about the pace of change, as they are always concerned about the risks involved in either a too slow or too rapid introduction of a new way of doing something. Present the pace of change as calculated to minimize the risk.

Written testimonials about either sort of impact help, but this kind of information can easily be massaged; Gartner reckoned that, by 2014, 10 to 15 per cent of social media reviews of products would be fake, so expect scepticism about your 'delighted' clients' reviews on your website to increase. Client satisfaction always improves after a good lunch. In 2010 a US news channel aired a story about how ratings algorithms had been manipulated. An individual paid the 'Better Business Bureau' in Santa Monica, California, $425 and succeeded in getting Hamas – a group that much of the US considers a terrorist organization – an A-minus rating. Similar services have been offered to authors for book reviews on Amazon (not this one!).

PERSONALIZE INFORMATION IN TERMS OF VALUES

Good salespeople know the promises that they can make about their solution: 'Saved 30 per cent of operating costs', 'Increased leads on average by 40 per cent with 20 per cent less effort', 'Reduced the cost of training by 20 per cent year on year over five years without affecting staff turnover'. Great salespeople choose the promises that excite them with which to excite their client. Why?

Selling takes lots of energy. You kiss a lot of frogs along the way to find your prince. Everybody knows this, so if you, the salesperson, are not excited and genuinely passionate about the outcomes for your clients, you will not make it. The number of frogs will simply overwhelm you and the words will turn to slime in your mouth.

Detailing the outcome(s) you find most inspiring starts with understanding what excites you. If you love solutions that are new, highlight how the outcome refreshes the organization and the people in it. If you love solutions that are immaculately engineered, highlight how the outcome creates a totally reliable sort of delivery. If you love beauty, tell the customer about how elegantly the process works, how simple it is to operate, how happy people are to use it. Most of all, tell them what *your* experience of using the solution has been like (you have to have taste before you can cook).

Of course, you may want to hold back from sharing why you are so passionate about the solution until you have worked out what motivates your customer around the idea of a solution. Their values and motives provide the energy for their decision, not yours. Often, the initial benefits they seek are not the main reasons for the purchase. Making shareholders richer is the job, but not what they really care about. Working out their real motivation is harder; you might have to disclose your passion first:

'Obviously, I believe in what our solutions can do for customers. But which of the potential outcomes we have been discussing are most interesting for you and your business?'

What sort of an answer will they give you? It might be something rational and impersonal, such as cost reduction, revenue increase or risk management. Then you might say:

'Yes, as a business that is the point of what we do. But personally... well, the thing I'm most proud about what we deliver is... a great opportunity to break away from all the legacy constraints and to really think again about how to capture more value for our client's customers in the process. [This is the salesperson's personal value: strategic advantage.] How about you? If we were to work with you on this, what would you like your legacy to be?'

If they still say cost reduction, revenue increase and the rest, you might have to adjust your enthusiasms. But mostly they will say something like:

'If it works, it would just give us such a great edge on our competitors. [Value: winning.] They are an arrogant bunch. I would rather like to hear from one of our spies that XYZ's Marketing Director's nose was firmly out of joint...'

Now you might make a mental note to put the price of a sector exclusivity deal in the draft contract.

Putting it all together

Knowing what you sell from the perspective of what the client values is different from knowing what you sell from your company's perspective. The most persuasive facts are always the ones that relate to your personal experience of the solution as a client, so it helps to have been a client of the solution you sell.

Functional knowledge matters for your credibility, but it may not be of much interest to all clients. Impact on performance and on the operation of the company is more critical. You need facts and figures about these aspects of the promise you make.

Finding out about what really motivates the individual client to change the way they do something takes time. Knowledge about personal benefits achieved by other clients may help them to open up.

16 CAMPAIGNS, NOT CRISES

'To win one hundred victories in one hundred battles is not the acme of skill. To subdue the enemy without fighting is the acme of skill.'

Sun Tzu

A target is not an action. Turning a target into campaigns makes it so. The above-average salesperson needs tactical skills that are also above average, not least to outwit the competition. Without these organized efforts, the work becomes unfocused and efforts are not rewarded.

These are the generic steps to take in a sales campaign:

1. Identify likely target clients and get to meet them.
2. Build relationships with leads (sponsors and stakeholders).
3. Qualify prospects (sponsors and stakeholders).
4. Clarify the scope of client needs and propose your solution/ service.
5. Negotiate.
6. Close.

Each of these steps requires planning and actions to move the opportunity through the sales 'funnel'. ('Funnel' refers to the item of cooking or garage equipment worn on the head of the Tin Woodman on the way to Oz, which you use to channel a diverse volume of fluid from a wide aperture through a narrow neck into a small opening such as a bottle, without losing a drop. The analogy with the sales cycle is more like the former than the latter...) Every business will have different ratios of funnel 'entrants' to sales closed, of solutions proposed to sales closed. This helps you decide how many campaigns you need to start. The ratio of cost of sales to value of sales (aka 'expense to bookings') also provides insights into campaigning. It certainly helps sales managers to compare the performance of members of the sales team.

Most sales organizations have formal lead tracking systems and meetings which good salespeople will often subvert, as they know a recorded 50 per cent chance of succeeding with a $2 million contract will be used to reassure anxious executives. Successful salespeople love to surprise their bosses and worry that declaring victory too early can backfire; if you raise the expectation of a $2 million win and it all goes pear-shaped, it will be all your fault... Better to seem less optimistic than the reality and have a reputation for secrecy.

ALWAYS BE READY TO ARTICULATE THE NEXT STEP UP OR DOWN THE FUNNEL

You can think about this in terms of the relationships with the clients and the task of achieving the goals of the sales campaign.

Relationships

The basic actions support a sequence of objectives:

1. To turn your lead into a prospect (a client with an identified need you can supply)
2. To turn that prospect into a qualified prospect (a client to whom you can supply a profitable solution)
3. To turn that qualified prospect into an active sponsor of a purchase
4. To build wider support for this purchase with other stakeholders (including procurement), so that a sale results.

This means different things at different stages. What do you need to do to make the prospect trust you? What do you need to do to get agreement with the prospect on the scope of their need (and your company's potential to help meet that need)? What do you need to do to get the prospect to find/divert/create the budget to pay for the solution?

Prospects' confidence in the idea of the solution and its value to them and their company will shift. This means that, as in the game of Snakes and Ladders, they can slide back or leap forwards in their readiness for the next step. Ladder actions aim to increase the customers' confidence in the service or solution (site visits, calls to/meetings with reference clients, demonstrations, meetings with delivery managers, specialists or project managers, board-level conference calls). Other ladder actions will increase their understanding of the value of this solution in use (third-party reviews, client satisfaction data, before/after benchmark studies, any positive internal reviews by technical buyers...).

Anticipating the snakes and averting their impact is also part of the continuous process of campaign review. Overall, your intention is to make the clients feel that your company provides a superior, open relationship and wants a superior, open relationship, and that there are very few, relatively harmless snakes on the board...

Tasks

Task-related actions are about the production and distribution of sales messages through the use of marketing collateral, proposals, cost estimates and the like.

The complexity of this communication increases as you go through the funnel, climaxing in the preparation of the proposal and/or pitch – and with it the costs. Even experienced salespeople underestimate the time needed to get internal approvals – legal, financial and so on – and to produce the final version on time. How good is your internal network at getting things approved (when the school holidays are happening...)?

Your ability to do this to a timetable you have proposed to the client (or which the client has set) is the test of your company's reliability. Late-delivered promises often rule you out of the running, so you need to build the sales team to guarantee that, if it comes to an all-nighter, they will support each other.

INCREASE THE TEMPO WHEN YOU NEED TO

Clients test your ability to deliver in the sales cycle by imposing deadlines. You might want to close the deal to coincide with the end of a quarter – clients also know this – or, more prosaically, because you have organized a holiday.

Here are some ideas for making things go faster if the client is hesitating or simply dragging their feet:

- Become a bit less patient. Talk about 'high sunk costs' to point out that you need the clients to move on. If you are in professional services, threaten (nicely) to send them an invoice for future time incurred.
- Introduce your ferocious boss into the mix: 'She's losing faith in this whole deal...' Play the sympathy card, if you think this will work.
- Draw up a timetable for decision-making, covering both sides of the deal and point out that, unless they get to second base in the next week, you could still be talking next year. (If this turns out to be their plan as there is nothing in the budget for this year, then reschedule...)
- Secure some sort of up-front commitment, preferably paid for. Most solutions are complex to put together but an agreement (signed) to go with your company, subject to price negotiation, might help. It also reduces the chance that they are also dragging their feet because of talking to competitors. This sort of deal can also include a timetable.

COOL THINGS DOWN TO RAISE THE STAKES

You might also need to slow things down. Sometimes the inexperience of the sponsor means that they are trying to foist an idea on a world that is either indifferent to the idea or, more probably, unaware of the importance of the change and its impact. Clients brimming with (misplaced) confidence in their ability to get things accepted – 'under the radar' is a favourite phrase which should ring alarm bells – are sometimes a liability to the salesperson; they may fail and you will have incurred some significant costs on their behalf.

And you might need to make the process more thoughtful and your client more deliberate. You could do this in one or more of the following ways.

- Run a workshop with a few less enthusiastic stakeholders who can be persuaded to join the campaign. Invite your sponsor to introduce the event.
- Discuss the change-management component of implementation: factors positively influencing the change and barriers to overcome. Explain that you need to have a balanced view of this in order to scope out the work properly. If they say 'That's our job', be sceptical.
- Hold off writing a proposal until you have spoken to end-users. A common misapprehension by impatient senior managers is that they understand and can represent the views of the stakeholders most likely to be affected; this is rarely true because the world has moved on since they were in the front line of operations.
- Hold off quoting a price until you have set up some options to test out their commitment and budget. Alternatively, ask them for their budget and propose a solution which fits this (they may really have complete decision-making authority).
- Ask to be paid for some aspect of the sales process: expenses for a 'feasibility study', perhaps. Once clients have to pay, they pay more attention.

Putting it all together

Many salespeople believe that life is too short for planning and, anyway, plans never turn out as you expect. Both these statements are true if your life is that of a surfing bum, and the second is true no matter what business you are in. But without a campaign and a plan, you have:

- no easy way to manage your boss, your team or your client
- no way of estimating or tracking cost of sales – and knowing when to withdraw
- nothing to review so that you can do better next time.

Plans also help you to make short cuts when you need to speed up, or to add activity when you need to slow things down. Upping the tempo is important to deal with competition; taking things easy helps the client to be more thoughtful about the scope.

17 LARGE SOLUTIONS NEED BROAD SUPPORT

'Those who are not with me are against me, and I crush anyone who stands against me!'
The Shredder, Teenage Mutant Ninja Turtles

Whether selling in or selling on, the constituency of support you enjoy from the wider organization or industry is critical. These are your references, your advocates and your critics. All successful salespeople pay great attention to cultivating their network; in any job it is part of the value they bring.

On specific bids, good salespeople distinguish **sponsors** – clients **respons**ible for deciding – from **stakeholders** – clients with a **stake** in the decision because they will be affected by it in some way. This makes stakeholders sound less committed, but this is not always the case. Stakeholders will not want to see their company make the wrong buying decision. While sponsors generally want to assist the process of change because have something to gain, stakeholders may resist, not just because they have much to lose but also because they fear the change is misguided. Great salespeople do not attempt to marginalize stakeholders until their motivations are clear.

Generally, there is a connection between the degree of consultation and the level of scepticism. Salespeople love a C-suite exec to be their sponsor, because, like the Shredder, they will use this authority to crush any opposing stakeholders. But this is often a bit of Ninja fantasy; the toughest sponsors are politically shrewd and like to share any potential blame in complex purchases. So they spread it around a bit and see if the sales team can come up with the goods to impress this diverse bunch of fence sitters and naysayers. Sophisticated clients see your ability to manage stakeholders in the sales process as a good test of how well you will manage them during the implementation.

UNDERSTAND THE LOWER-LEVEL STAKEHOLDERS IN THE ORGANIZATION

Managing the politics of decision-making starts with understanding the range of people involved. You will know whom your solution touches and you will also know what sort of organizational changes it involves. When the moment is right and your sponsoring client seems to be sufficiently interested to allow you access to information about current practice, suggest that you should also involve other people. Get hold of an organization chart or a list of people in the departments who are most likely to be affected. Your potential sponsor may brief you on who they are and how they are likely to feel about either the sale or the outcome, but it is worth finding out more in person.

Your aim is to get a picture of *their* attitude to the outcomes implied by your solution. Are they feeling positive or negative about the possibility of this change? Are they likely to be active or passive in their expression of these feelings? If active, what are they likely to do? How much influence do they have? The actively negative ones – the blockers – are likely to head your list of stakeholders to deal with, but generally these will be a minority; in most change situations approximately 50 per cent of people will be passive about what is being proposed and fewer than 25 per cent will actively obstruct the process.

It is often hard to get an appointment with blockers as they try to avoid having to state their objections, so it is best to leave these meetings until last. Start with the drivers – those stakeholders who, like the sponsor, are positive and will be active about helping to achieve the outcome. Then meet the passive group – supporters and those who are passively negative. Finally, meet the blockers, by which time you will know more about their objections.

Summarize the range of views and present the summary to your potential sponsor(s). This is often valuable in itself. It also helps if your current sponsor allows you to send a short version back to all the stakeholders you have involved. Speaking the truth to power gives you credibility, because power is not stupid or as out of touch as people imagine; they just don't have to confront the truth that often. Often the good news – '80 per cent of the people we met are longing for the system to be improved' – is more persuasive than the bad: 'There is currently between a 40 and 60 per cent error rate in the attribution of costs to budgets.' Highlight the comparative strengths of this company compared to others you have dealt with. Do not make things sound easier or simpler than they really are on the basis that 'the senior management team don't have much time to consider things in detail' or other such nonsensical reasons. If detail is required, then detail is what you give them – as a potential supplier you are not courting popularity with the sponsors, even if the stakeholders sometimes are.

Tempting though it may be, never rat on any stakeholder who has provided you with wonderful information in confidence; they will get you back if you win the contract. But when there are unsung heroes and heroines in the organization battling with the existing 'solution', highlight their magnificence. Praising people never hurts. Blaming people never works. So attribute the good stuff, if in doubt.

CHECK HOW FAR THE SPONSOR NEEDS CONSENSUS TO AGREE

Some sponsors will be afraid of tackling any negative response from the stakeholders, so make sure that your proposal allows for dissent – call it 'dialogue' – and deals with it as part of the proposed project plan. Others will see your sales process as a golden opportunity to knock heads together, get stakeholders to fess up to their real concerns and generally come clean about what they really feel and think about any proposed changes. Braver sponsors might be up for a 'workshop' to air some of the views; and then ride roughshod over the worries. Less brave sponsors might want a feasibility study as a first step to build consensus.

In some organizations it is the senior stakeholders who are the issue. A board at war with itself is never an easy backdrop to a large solution purchase, unless the solution can miraculously solve the source of irritation. A major systems upgrade which will open up doors between siloed departments sounds like an easy win, but in practice can lead to senior managers manning the battlements of their personal citadels over the functions they expect to see. Sometimes time can be your friend and encouraging people to debate may reveal the factions to them.

For this reason, it is always worth trying to understand how decisions work in the client organization. Does the CEO decide on all major cross-departmental actions? Or does the organization prefer to delay the decision rather than risk blood on the boardroom carpet? Some organizations are still military in the way they manage power, but increasingly the impact of technology is breaking down hierarchical barriers and larger organizations are becoming more democratic in the way they decide on strategies, solutions and systems.

Very rarely does the job title give you any real insight into the process of stakeholders' involvement in decision-making. 'Senior technical advisers' may have less impact on key decisions than the sponsor's executive coach. I worked for a large grocery chain that had installed expensive merchandising cabinets containing exotic cooking ingredients. Sales were poor and profit margins worse. When questioned about this decision, there would be an embarrassed silence, until it was revealed as the Chairman's wife's idea.

BUILD YOUR WIDER NETWORK IN THE CLIENT'S INDUSTRY

Reputations count when making big decisions. If you and your company have a good reputation with the wider market, then things are a bit easier. This is less about marketing than references. Existing clients are often helpful in this regard but so are disinterested third parties who would give you a reference: academics, other suppliers who have a good working relationship with your target client, or major shareholders.

The personal narratives of previous clients are often the most influential, especially if the topic or the client is new. 'Don't ask me, ask my customer' is much stronger than '90 per cent of our customers would recommend us' or even '90 per cent of our new customers – like you – come through referral'. New clients like the chance to interrogate another client – as long as this other customer is not a direct competitor. Naturally, you do not give out any contact details without consulting the previous customer first, but when you provide three references for your solution, then you will have achieved more than setting up three reference calls or meetings. You are also consolidating your network.

Prepare your referees to give the right information. Tell them what you are discussing with the new client, and what you have told them about your work in their company. Imagine what you would want to know as the new client. You'd want information about the situation the previous clients found themselves in, why they wanted a solution, why they chose your company and what had changed as a result – not how many trillion terabytes of storage were involved but, more broadly, 'Did it work?' You might also enquire what it had cost, how long the change had taken and what they would advise you to beware of when dealing with Acme Solutions PLC. Always encourage your referees to be honest, detailing how you handled problems. As with any review, '90 per cent great and 120 per cent committed' is more believable than '100 per cent'.

Putting it all together

Adjust proposals to reflect what you hear from stakeholders. Crushing opposition is tempting to all, but usually the cockroach gets its revenge by soiling your sandwich at a later stage. Much better to demonstrate that you have listened, reflected and adjusted (albeit in a small way) what you are going to offer.

Involve some of the stakeholders in the delivery process. Use steering committees of the great and the good (basically sponsors and supporters), with just a sprinkling of the disaffected. Suddenly, the disaffected stakeholders find themselves in a minority, even though (perhaps) they represent a huge constituency that believes the same thing as they do.

18 THE BRAND IS YOU

'There's only one word that is banned in our company: brand.
We are only as good as our latest product. I don't believe in
brand at all.'

James Dyson

There's a dream that your brand as a B2B provider will make the selling into order taking, with a bit of negotiation thrown in. But relying on brand alone will only get you into the room...

'An ex-McKinsey partner was hired by a start-up B2B services business I worked for in the hope that his profile would release a flood of sales. He never sold a single contract. The "no brand" start-up just wasn't McKinsey (and he, sadly, was no salesman).'

At the higher end of the service food chain – the professional services firms – you buy the people involved in the delivery of the service. They must embody your firm's brand values. Most professional firms use the name of a founder to communicate this fact. But the heritage of the company also matters in terms of the client's perception of the risk. This is why successful individual professionals often find it hard – as the ex-McKinsey partner did – to leverage off their own relationships and get access. As the 'face' of a company with no such legacy, your clients may not assume that your standards automatically apply to others in a firm of lesser pedigree.

A solution can build a reputation, be differentiated and enjoy loyalty and longevity in the market, just as a professional can. Building a story around the history of the solution is part of building that mystique.

'This solution is currently about 35 per cent of our worldwide revenues and this percentage has continued to grow despite the downturn. There are now more than 40 international customers who have continued to invest in the solution over the last six years. We're very proud of what they have managed to do with it. It's delivering for them.'

This sort of solution-brand reputation might even attract new customers' interest. A well-established, carefully marketed procedure – like laser eye surgery – can attract clients as much as a well-known ophthalmologist or physician.

Does the same thing apply in B2B? Each business situation is unique, but the brand of either your firm or your solution enables you to make a noise in the market and attract attention, even interest. But for someone to actually want to buy your solution, its backstory must be relevant to their ambition. It is the marrying of the capabilities of the solution with outcomes they want to achieve that turns interest into desire. Your brand reputation may give you access, a place on a tendering list, but does not guarantee the sale.

DO NOT ASSUME THEY THINK YOU ARE WORTH ANYTHING

The first lesson when working for a well-known brand is humility. You have been well trained, no doubt, and have many ways to demonstrate your company's value. The client's expectations will be high for this reason, but they may also be sceptical. Young professionals and young salespeople can struggle with being credible, no matter what their business card. They do not know as much about business as the client; they have had less experience, less time to make mistakes and acquire a point of view.

Even grey hairs are no guarantee that you will be seen as valuable – although looking a bit older than you are seems to help. The answer is preparation; research and analysis are substitutes for wisdom. Interesting hypotheses, fresh ideas, a real attempt to understand what is going on in *their* industry, with *their* customers, with *their* competition, with *their* business performance... not only are these interesting, but they show a degree of dedication to the client in advance of the meeting.

Going empty-headed is risky. You will be negatively affecting your company's brand. When you have something interesting to say about the client's business – not just your solution – then, as the salesperson, you feel more confident. This has nothing to do with experience or age. Youth has its own advantages: energy, fresh thinking unfettered by too much experience, a hunger to succeed. Age can reflect on what it has seen elsewhere. Brand means you are on a list, but not the shortlist.

DEVELOP YOUR PERSONAL PROFILE IN LINE WITH YOUR COMPANY'S POSITIONING

Great salespeople are experts in at least two dimensions: their client's industry and its issues; and their solution and its outcomes.

'When I'm describing how the solution will work, I often get a great feeling of power when I can really nail how it is designed to work in their context. You can see clients from the business waiting in judgement to see how the techies have "failed" to understand the real business issues. You can see the technical people in the audience waiting to catch you out on some detail. If you can avoid both these pitfalls and demonstrate that this not only will work but will transform the way that the customer works for ever, you win. The test of your mastery of both technology and context is the way you show you understand change...'

What is your individual USP? Where are your areas of expertise that differentiate you from the other salespeople your client talks to? With time, it helps to develop your own image within your company and also within the market, based on your interests and career experience. Internally, you can do this by setting up online communities or chat rooms of people with similar interests, or by arranging for meetings on topics that interest you. Externally, you can do this by blogging, talking at conferences, possibly with PR. If the client sees you as somebody with an area of independent specialist expertise in addition to your role as a salesperson, they may listen differently to you. You are still a chameleon, but one with a preferred colour.

Obviously, this needs to be thought through in terms of the impact on the client's perception of your brand. Developing your profile as a crazy boffin works if your company's positioning is leading-edge technology, but not if your brand image is sober reliability. If you are reading this as a person who started out as the specialist or line manager and have moved into sales, you will recognize the importance of this individual profiling as a client; salespeople who cannot add value in person are just a waste of your time. The sooner they show you the product the better.

Your aim is to make sure that they are glad that they chose your company to talk with, rather than the competition – and to make yourself memorable.

BRAND MAY AFFECT THEIR PERCEPTION OF PRICE

A no-brand offer is often expected to be cheaper than one from an established company. Most professional firms take at least seven years to build a positive reputation so, if you are just starting out, you may need to emphasize other things in your personal history which suggest that the client will be getting a great deal if they work with your company: your colleagues' track records with several blue-chip firms and/or technical expertise out of the lab of a top university. You can also emphasize the way in which the solution has been developed and tested – suggesting not only a rigorous but also lengthy process of investment.

A well-known brand will, however, have less difficulty justifying its fees. Professional services firms provide some ideas here, too, as a salesman who works a lot in this sector told me:

'McKinsey want people who can contribute to clients' business and who have impact. They don't like the terminology associated with selling, preferring more neutral terms like "partnering". When young principals [the career stage before being given a business development role] are being tested for partner potential, they give them a budget for a specific client and then, after 9–12 months, go and ask the clients they have been "contributing" to to assess the benefit they have brought. If these outcomes are in line with McKinsey's (very high) fee rates, then they consider the person seriously for the partnership.'

This is really ensuring that your brand is worth the premium price, but the principle seems to be correct. Assessing value after the solution has been installed is about not just how far it 'did what it said on the tin', but also about assessing the ultimate value of the outcomes delivered. What if your client got this wrong? Your solution could deliver and yet the value perception might be less than expected. A brand worth the premium not only tracks benefits but has a point of view about the value of those benefits during the sales process.

Putting it all together

Brand is important because it creates expectations and interest and can be a substitute for client experience. Because information about your performance as a company is more readily available, a well-known brand now guarantees less in terms of an easier time in the sales funnel than it did. 'You are really only as good as your last job', as one salesperson suggested, paraphrasing the Hollywood cliché. That being said, if you profile yourself carefully as a specialist and develop a point of view about how your solutions best deliver value, your clients may expect to pay a bit more for your service than for your competitors'.

19 ASSUMPTIONS COMMUNICATE AS MUCH AS ASSERTIONS

*'Ninety per cent of selling is conviction and
ten per cent is persuasion.'*
Shiv Khera

Although face to face is where business really happens,
preparatory work is also important, as this makes the meeting
more productive for all concerned. Every solutions provider
will have messages that they want to communicate about their
company and their offerings, but often a more oblique approach
works better, particularly when it appears to be based on the
assumption that you and your products are of high quality,
reliable and so on.

Think of a CV. When a person says they are 'an excellent team
player', what do you as the potential employer think? Laying
claim to qualities as an individual or a company rarely works
and may have the opposite effect; buyers like to make their own
judgements about the individual's qualities. Now think about
how you would communicate in a CV that you were a good team
player. You would use the word 'we' frequently when listing your
achievements, making generous reference to others' contributions
to your advancement. You would cite achievements that were
about the building or maintenance of teams and the motivation and
development of others. This modesty would communicate that you
could lead and influence others to perform, which, in most senior
jobs, would be seen as an advantage. You *assume*, in the way you
write your CV, that teamworking is a natural attribute of all people
working at your level.

How can you use this idea of using assumptions, not assertions, in the way you manage the pre-meeting communications with a targeted client?

UNDERSTAND THE THREE MAIN MARKETING MESSAGES ABOUT YOUR BRAND

Know what your company stands for in terms of its unique selling proposition as the provider of B2B solutions. Do you represent better value, quality, technical reliability, range, a degree of innovation?

These are the three most common 'messages' for most solutions/ B2B services businesses:

- It works – we deliver more value than we claim. (This is the credibility element in trust.)
- We are easy to do business with. (This is the chemistry element of trust.)
- We will work very hard for you. (This is the reliability and commitment element of trust.)

Your company will probably be more refined about such matters than these rather bald assertions, but clarity about what assumptions you make about yourself as a solution provider matters, as individually salespeople may have other values and interests which they might inadvertently leak out in the way they communicate with clients, especially at the start of the sales process where clients are observing them most closely. Being pushy doesn't work with professional services, for example.

SHAPE YOUR COMMUNICATION TO MAKE YOUR ATTRIBUTES CLEAR

The most powerful way to communicate a set of values or attributes in an assumptive way is when you say no. This can happen at any stage in the sales process and changes the dialogue with your client, as the following examples show.

- 'It's one of our rules for doing business; we won't write a client a proposal unless...'
- 'We have learned from clients in the past that, although what you are now asking for is genuinely what you want, it won't actually deliver unless...'
- 'I wouldn't want to give you a snap answer to that question without some proper analysis. It won't take long, but in this situation speed is not the only criterion for excellence. I'll look at what you have sent me and give you a reply by the end of the week.'

One salesperson for a specialist consulting business refuses to write a proposal until she has met at least three people in addition to the sponsor – generally their boss, a peer and a direct report. Her reasoning (shared openly) is that all clients are to some extent blindsided in their diagnosis of the issues and it is easy to waste a lot of time and money working on the wrong definition of the problem. If the client cannot give her this access as part of the sales process, then she won't bid unless there is clear evidence of such an internal consultation process, which has preceded their involvement. Her company turns down all RFP bids unless they are allowed to meet a sample of people and form their own judgement.

Although initially such 'rules' may look hard for the salesperson, they can make things easier, too; as with any criteria, they enable the salesperson to make a quick decision and they also mean that the client will not approach the company unless they broadly agree with working in this way. Done supportively, declaring such assumptions reassures the client about the credibility of these manufacturing experts. This company doesn't charge for the interviews either, which underlines their view that this is part of selling, not delivery. Interestingly, they fell into this method of scoping projects because they made a lot of costly mistakes by not ratifying individual briefs in this way. They tell the stories of these mistakes as a way to convince their clients that this free process of consultation is necessary for a good proposal. Clients seem to like the fact that others then get to see the consultants before any decision to hire is taken; try before you buy.

REINFORCE THE MESSAGES WITH GOOD INTERPERSONAL BEHAVIOUR

The biggest mistake you can make at the first meeting is always the smallest one; it might be a client name continuously mispronounced, an inability to pick up on clues that the potential sponsor is giving you about how to handle one of their colleagues in the meeting, or a general lack of social subtlety. All these things may prevent you from being allowed to progress further. The 'rules' for this are really the same as those that apply to being a good guest:

- **Arrive punctually** so that nobody is kept waiting. But if your 'host' is still busy, wait without resentment. This often means allowing more time before the next call than you might, so that you aren't checking your watch the whole time.
- **Dress appropriately.** This will be covered later, but sober is better than loud, unless your service is something about design or style. You want to be able to melt into the background and let the client shine during most first meetings.
- **Bring a gift.** PowerPoint as a present lacks imagination, but if your message is predictability – 'what you see is what you get' – PowerPoint is good. If the meeting takes your client away from her lunch, you might suggest you bring sandwiches or, over morning coffee, some pastries. Whatever the gift, being thoughtful matters far more than being lavish. In fact, 'lavish' might communicate 'unaffordable' to some clients. The best gift is a stimulating conversation backed up with information the client can use to look good.
- **Show an interest in other guests** and entertain them. If you are meeting a group, the tendency will be to focus on the client rather than her team. But even if one person is the ultimate decision-maker, they wouldn't be involving members of their team if they weren't going to be consulted. Your ability to socialize with everyone is important. You are being watched. What would you be like to work with? Dialogue and discussion matter more than any material facts in most first meetings. Why would a customer invite a windbag back to puff some more?

- **Don't outstay your welcome** and run over the agreed time. If you agreed that you would take an hour, take an hour and no longer. Chances are they all have other meetings, so finishing five minutes early is even better. If the meeting started late, check how much time they really have and adapt what you have planned accordingly. Organizations vary hugely in how good they are at timekeeping, so even if someone says, 'Let's carry on; we can afford to be late for the weekly conference call with X', reschedule a second meeting; this level of casualness about time (and therefore cost) is not what you stand for. (It may tell you something about doing business with their company.) Don't make them feel bad about their casualness; indicate that you find it refreshing and that multitasking is the way forward. Potentially, make some disparaging remarks about your own company and its excessive attention to such details. But don't run over time.

Putting it all together

The way you set up the meeting and behave when you meet creates opportunities to demonstrate behaviour associated with a set of assumptions about business and doing business with others.

You need to know what differentiates your company in terms of values and offering and then consider how this translates in terms of behaviour with the clients at the early stages of the relationship. While you have to adapt to your clients to some extent, you also have to be clear about your own standards and prepared to walk away if the client does not understand or accept this.

Using your behaviour to communicate what you stand for is better than telling the client what you stand for.

20 AGENDA BUILDING IS RELATIONSHIP BUILDING

'If I had to identify in one word the reason why the human race has not achieved, and never will achieve, its full potential, that word would be "meetings".'
Dave Barry

There is a world of difference between the preparation you do and the preparation you show. The goal of most early meetings is to build a sufficiently trusting relationship with a stranger for them to disclose something of their situation, which might become an opportunity for your company.

Although both parties know this is the name of the game, the degree of disclosure often reflects who has initiated the meeting. Where the client has suggested you meet, you can expect the session to be an exchange of information: what we do, what you might need – but preferably in the reverse order. Of course, this isn't always the case. The client may simply be fishing for information – about a competitor you work for, say – or just educating themselves about something you know about. If they are 'fishing', they will be asking all the questions, so you will have limited time to do some fishing yourself.

Where the client has allowed you entry to their business, on your initiative, it is usually because you have offered some inducement, which is sufficiently sweet for them to see the hour as valuable. It might be analysis or the chance to meet the author of a well-received report. The idea of baiting the hook with some intellectual property – a benchmark study, the provisional specification of an upgraded system from the one they have – is that, while they are munching, you are cross-examining them to find out what higher-value needs they might have to which you can supply a solution. The stimulus package therefore has to be not only about information but also about data gathering.

In both these cases – and there are many others – the key is to agree an agenda that meets both your expectations and those of the client.

DECIDE WHAT YOU WANT TO KNOW

You may have a list of qualification criteria for clients, some of which will have been ticked in the preliminary scrutiny of targets. Often, these criteria are about your solution, but they may also be about competition in the account, availability of budget, openness to a longer-term relationship and so on. Many of these can be assessed only when you are meeting the lead.

You will also want to get some information about the current 'solution' the client is using. When you are invited in this is usually easy to come by, but when you initiate the meeting there can be a whiff of 'That's ours to know and yours to find out...' The blinds may come down on anything strategically important until you have signed a non-disclosure agreement.

Once you have a list of what you think is reasonable to learn on the first meeting – and not in the public domain already – then you frame an agenda around topics that will lead you to discuss these aspects of their business. For example, suppose you need to find out about their annual spend on information systems in your area; stimulus material about improving value for money about information systems might be appropriate. They will know what the game is, but if your thesis was 'Those spending more than 500 million have to tackle efficiency improvement in a different way from those spending 300 million or less', they will more or less have to indicate which camp they are in when they agree or disagree with your analysis.

DESIGN THE AGENDA

When you have your list of things you are interested in, you need to lay it to one side and consider what the target might find of interest. One successful salesperson explained their process like this:

'It's a good idea to give a lead some options about what might be on the agenda for a first meeting. There are always a number of things we can talk about based on our experience, but making the client choose what they would find valuable is a good start to finding out about the areas where they have interests. Sometimes they are just looking for a bit of edutainment to brighten a dull meeting, so whatever you do mustn't be too earnest at the start. "An interactive session on…" usually gets a positive response, especially when you frame it as exploring answers to questions. I always suggest a set of questions, which their company might reasonably be expected to have an interest in answering. This sometimes provokes a list of other questions in return – the ones they are *really* facing – and so we then know what's more/less engaging for the client or team we are meeting. I see the point of these meetings as the start of a dialogue with multiple points of contact, so the agenda always ends with "What next?" or, perhaps more subtly, "What are the implications for us from this session today?"'

This preliminary attempt at dialogue is not always successful – people are too busy perhaps to really engage before you arrive. Successful salespeople will always confirm the agenda at the start of the meeting and adapt – insofar as they can – depending on the outcome. For this reason, any slide deck does not need necessarily to have a narrative; it often works better when each slide raises a discrete issue and you can show them in an order that suits your client.

While there are no generic agendas for first meetings, the following should always be covered:

- **Who we are.** Both sides introduce themselves (but not necessarily their company in a huge amount of detail – that becomes important where there is a deal to be done). Include background, experience, previous clients – credibility-building stuff – in a few sentences. If you can't address your credibility in five sentences, 15 will only make things worse.
- **What we want from this meeting.** 'Contracting' about the meeting agenda is a prelude to the behaviours you will revisit

when you contract about the project or the specification of the solution. Behaviourally, it is identical; good contracts require both parties to be open about their needs and expectations rather than their positions (client/vendor). Your needs are to find a way to do business with them, based on your understanding more about their business and what it needs. The client's objectives are often less clear; it might be information or the need to satisfy the person who asked them to see you... The key parts of any contract are deliverable and deadline, so check these out with respect to the meeting as well.

- **Something of value to the client.** Gifts create obligations to reciprocate, so the salesperson needs to demonstrate value in the first meeting. As stated elsewhere, this needs to be about the client rather than the salesperson's company or solutions.
- **Next steps.** Many clients just want to leave things at one meeting, and not necessarily because the salesperson didn't impress. No client is ever entirely in control of their environment, so even if they like you or what you have to say or have found the meeting interesting, they may not immediately want to meet you again next week/month. This puts salespeople – who are usually motivated to find and close business to a deadline – in a fix. Push or wait? Pushing puts the relationship at risk; waiting puts the opportunity at risk. The main thing is to continue the dialogue with this client or others so that the meeting is not wasted. The timetable is less important – ultimately. Salespeople recognize what has been a good meeting and have faith that it will pay off, somehow, some day. They push on, continuing the discussion relentlessly but to the client's timetable.

FIND OUT WHAT'S REALLY ON THEIR MIND

In solutions selling, with all its complexity of stakeholders, valuable outcomes and organizational change, you are not necessarily controlling a linear process, but an iterative one. What are often called 'objections' in classic product selling are often real problems for the solutions client (and opportunities to enlarge the solution offered).

For example, when we initiate a meeting with an agenda about, say, the missed opportunity our solution represents, the client may well agree, but say, 'I love the idea, but sadly your timing isn't great', because the company has just completed a three-year strategic review and the board has decided their future lies in a rather different direction. The average salesperson will not be put off; she still wants a strategic conversation so that the opportunity represented by their solution is at least considered. She would push for this.

However, according to successful salespeople, 'bad timing' is often code for 'politics I can't influence'. So the next step is to help the client with that influence rather than continue to push the strategic conversation at the next meeting, which is doomed to failure. Find out the board's strategic agenda, find out the changes this will necessitate and then consider how your company's know-how can assist. The end goal may be a large solution sale but the short-term goal is now to be part of the strategic implementation process, which will provide information and relationships in support of that longer-term goal. And it will provide support for the client opposite you. As one salesperson put it, 'I stick with where they are before I try to take them somewhere else.'

The agenda for the next meeting is now about your experience of supporting strategic change – using the tools, skills and experience of doing this in the past. Helping *is* selling.

Putting it all together

Building an agenda helps identify a sponsor's interests and demonstrates a service orientation. These interests may emerge at any time: when you are agreeing the questions they wish the initial meeting to address, during the meeting, or when you are formulating the agenda for the next steps at the end. While this personal agenda may not match the one you would ideally like for your solution to find a place to put down roots, there are often ways to add value to the relationship with the lead and then to get further introductions to others whose agendas align more with yours. The key is to stimulate dialogue about issues, opportunities and solutions – yours and theirs.

21 FIRST MEETINGS TEST YOUR STATUS

'People like people like themselves.'
Tony Robbins

As social animals we like to live in groups, and as we live in groups relative status matters. Status does not just mean job titles and the number of direct reports you control. It also means the way you behave. We are often particularly aware of this on first meeting people, because biologically we are assessing the 'threat' of the 'stranger'.

In terms of client relationships, this is a crucial moment for building trust. Just as statistics about non-verbal communication are popularized, so are those about how we make decisions to trust others. Whichever source you believe, it seems likely that this decision takes just a few minutes, depending on different propensities we have as personalities. Although we can modify the impression we create over time, a bad start is a bad start, so, if there is an opportunity to manage this well, good salespeople do so:

'The nerves are something you get used to. When I started, I spent a lot of time in company toilets and avoiding coffee before meetings. Although I was "carrying the bag", I felt in awe of these captains of industry we were calling on and of my boss's polished way of dealing with them.'

Neuroscience suggests that the brain reacts to perceived threats in a fraction of a second by changing the chemistry in our heads. This, in turn, affects our ability to think rationally. A number of factors cause the 'threat' responses – fight, flight or freeze. One of them is the client's sense that the new person is threatening their status. This is partly because the salesperson, like any newcomer, is not 'one of us' and unfamiliarity is inherently a cause for concern. But it is also to do with behaviour.

How do clients behave on first meeting? They may stand up slowly from behind the desk, extending the hand of greeting at arm's length, talking rather loudly perhaps and extensively – a slightly larger-than-life version of the person you subsequently get to know. The reason is that all these behaviours are associated with raising their relative status, confronted by a person they do not know. Your tendency may be to do likewise and it is important to match but not confront the status difference with your client:

'The CEO's office was the entire top floor of a building in the West End of London. You stepped out of the lift and there were three receptionists at the desk facing you, one of whom walked you to the door of what I assumed was his office. Along the way we passed through three anterooms each decorated in a different style: Chinese antiques, medieval European antiques and modern Italian furniture. When I commented on these to the receptionist, she explained that her boss's wife was an interior designer. At the office door we were greeted by the personal assistant and shown into another room with two other administrative staff. This was a rather cramped room with three desks for the assistants and two chairs for visitors facing them. The personal assistant offered the usual drink, and said that the CEO was "in conference". I sat awkwardly in my heavy overcoat for at least ten minutes until a light on her desk went on and she said, "Dr Busetti will see you now."

'There was another door at the end of the room and, my heart beating rather fast, I went through it. I found myself in the largest office I have ever seen. On the opposite side of the room was an antique desk (Signora Busetti's choice, no doubt), behind which sat a slight man on the phone. He indicated I should approach, which I did; it was all of 20 paces across this gigantic empty space. As I got nearer he smiled broadly and apologetically, held out his hand, still talking on the phone, and indicated that I should sit down in the chair opposite his desk. It looked like a very low chair so I decided to take off my coat and place it on the chair and headed for the conference table close by. I wasn't going to be intimidated any more.'

DO NOT BE INTIMIDATED BY A SENIOR CLIENT'S STATUS

Status is communicated by people's posture, their voice, their facial expression and even their breathing. The higher your status the more you fill space and time; you stand upright with your chin up, you speak slowly and deliberately, you make direct eye contact and you smile, you breathe regularly and deeply. You behave as if you are unafraid. If you want to lower your status, you sit and cross your legs or arms (this protects the more vulnerable parts of your body); you incline your head; you speak quietly and perhaps rather fast; you avoid direct eye contact and your breathing is irregular. You are behaving as if you expect to be attacked.

One way to get control is to change your own thinking about the encounter. If you are convinced that you can help this organization with your company's services and competence, you will behave differently than if you are worried about the outcome of the meeting in terms of failing to get an order. Junior or younger salespeople often find it hard to do this, as they are excited and concerned about their own performance. If you can focus on helping the client with your ideas, you reduce their status in your mind; they are just another client that you would like to assist in improving their business.

Match eye contact, firmness of handshake and tone of voice, and allow the client the space and time to feel that they can dominate the situation, but not you. One rule of thumb you might consider is never to interrupt your client until they feel comfortable with you.

MODULATE YOUR STATUS TO GET THE RESPONSE YOU WANT

Once you have mastered the general principle of status behaviour, you can learn to use it to your advantage.

If there is someone who seems reluctant to talk, lower your status. When presenting, you can do this easily by sitting down. This raises the status of everybody else in the room (who are already sitting down, we assume) and indicates that you want them to 'take the floor'. You can apply this to an individual by using silence. If you want them to say more or to talk at a less superficial level, you leave space and time for them to do so. When we say nothing we reduce our status, and this means that the other person's status is raised.

If the person is not interested, raising your status can have a big impact. Many of the salespeople interviewed for this book said, 'You have to be prepared to walk away', which is another way of indicating that you will no longer accept a subordinate status with your client. You stand up, you turn your back on them (a very high-status thing to do as it indicates that you do not see them as a threat), and you prepare to leave. This is often a last-ditch attempt to gain ground, but there are lesser variations that may get the lead's attention:

- Increasing the intensity of your gaze – this might involve looking up suddenly in response to what they have said or to their silence
- Increasing your hand gestures – pointing things out – literally and metaphorically – increases your status, as when passing a document across the table (invading their space)
- Speaking a thought out loud, slowly and deliberately – 'Really? *Really?*' This is short of an insult, but clearly indicates that their reaction is less than you expect.
- Leaning forward in your chair – or leaning well back, looking at the ceiling.

These sorts of behaviours are provocations to respond, small assaults on the client's apparent complacency, so be prepared for a reaction in kind.

MATCH YOUR STATUS TO THEIRS AS THE MEETING ENDS

Often, it will take the whole meeting for the client to feel comfortable with you – comfortable enough to introduce you to their boss or another person, or indeed to host a second meeting. As representatives of product suppliers, salespeople are encouraged to see the sale as what matters and that your job is to be whatever the customer needs you to be to achieve this goal. High-value solutions representatives should not think like this; for their offering to be valued, they too must be valued by the client. In status terms, this means that the final impression after the first meeting must be that you – and your company – are the client's equal in status terms.

At the end of the meeting there is always the 'next steps' discussion, where both parties agree what action to take. First, it is important to conclude the session with a professional summary of what you have covered, any agreements that have been reached and any areas that remain 'open' and unresolved. The client will often welcome your taking control of the agenda, as long as your summary accurately reflects their feelings about the meeting; you have earned the right to be equal status by this point.

Secondly, you need to assess how they are feeling about the issue and manage the status accordingly. If the meeting has revealed that the client is both highly anxious and insecure, then you would probably ask – low status – 'What would you like me to do as a result of this meeting?' or – higher status – 'Where will you take this next?' If they seem confident that the meeting has been productive, then you might frame the question in a more equal-status way, looking them in the eye and saying, 'So what should we do next?'

Thirdly, final impressions are as important to manage as the first few minutes in status terms. As you put things into a bag or put on your coat, express appreciation for their time and for the information they have given you and indicate how you will be in touch again. Be the first to offer your hand this time.

Putting it all together

Being aware of the difference in status between you as the salesperson and your client is one thing. Using this difference is a skill. Great salespeople are continuously experimenting with the relative status between them and their clients to ensure a positive outcome from the meeting. This is not because what you say doesn't matter. It is in addition to having good questions and clear messages to communicate. You mustn't either threaten your client's status or be too subordinate to her. The aim is to gradually match your status so that by the end they see you as an equal they can do business with.

22 COMMON GROUND CREATES RAPPORT

'The snake which cannot cast its skin has to die. As well the minds which are prevented from changing their opinions; they cease to be minds.'
Friedrich Nietzsche

Salespeople are the 'outsiders', which means they always have a challenge being accepted into an organization. To do this they have to build a connection between themselves and the client and eventually between the two companies. Trained salespeople use a combination of techniques: matching client language, mirroring their behaviour and finding common interests. Excellent salespeople manage to do this without the client noticing. In other words, they have become unconsciously competent at building rapport and other people don't notice what they are doing. They just appear to be 'our kind of person', even though they are outsiders.

Great salespeople do this without effort. They just blend in with whomever they are facing; as a researcher they put you at your ease, they appear open and build on any connection that exists – for example, the person who effected the introduction. If you ask them how they do this, you get a range of replies, but most come back to the same point. 'We share a common humanity that is actually more important than company culture, goals or roles. My job is to focus on this aspect first.'

Quite a few of the successful salespeople I met were not the standard good-looking, well-groomed types that people expect. Several had minor disabilities, which they had evidently learned to overcome. Perhaps being different from other people had taught them to subordinate aspects of themselves and really concentrate on the client so that their difference – their disability – disappeared. It may also be that the disability helped to generate a base level of sympathy in the client, which they were able to build on. When somebody really engages with you, you forget their wheelchair and, when you do remember it, you are doubly impressed.

How do you achieve this chameleon-like ability to blend in with the culture of the company you are visiting? Although the skills face to face are important, particularly your ability to pick up on the way the people in the company relate to one another, it starts with research into their culture – the values, behaviours and ways of working that are their 'normal'.

OBSERVE YOUR CLIENT FOR COMMON INTERESTS

'I'd love a coffee, thanks. Decaf, if possible. We were just commenting as we were sitting downstairs that you've got the latest Nespresso machines. They're much better, aren't they?' Does this sort of comment work at building rapport? As with everything in selling, if you are doing it inauthentically, then, no, it will sound inauthentic. If you once worked as a rep for Nespresso and are conditioned to notice coffee machines, it possibly might, if you reveal the fact.

A more natural way to do this is in the introductions. You have shaken hands – connected superficially – and accepted the offer of a drink, or not, commented on the weather, the traffic or the headline on the TV news in Reception and now you need to get to know one another. Order-taking salespeople had ample opportunity to do this while filling in some nonsense form about the car you might be thinking of buying. Solutions salespeople have to be upfront about establishing the relationship because many of their services will directly affect the person they are dealing with.

'Shall we start with some brief introductions?' This is the cold-call moment but face to face, so keep it short and relevant and use anything you have seen or heard about the person (social media details, LinkedIn, press) in what you say. 'Here's my card. Do you know what ABC does...? [Await the response and be prepared to give a one-sentence answer.] I've been a senior business developer with the company for three really interesting years, and I specialize in helping our clients with [choose the 'bait' topic you have contacted them about] although I once... [mention something in your past that you have in common]. I'm married with two school-age sons. What about you?'

Usually, people respond to the cues you have given them – duration of employment, job responsibilities, family situation in this case – so you can vary your introduction depending on how open you think they might be. (The family information is a calculated gamble, but not if there are family photos on the client's desk.) The lead then introduces themselves, and you have the chance to link their answers to yourself – either something you have said, such as a discussion of the relative age of your children – or something they say that you can relate to. In training courses we have found that total strangers can find three areas of common interest in about five minutes; this is usually because markets are actually quite homogenous in terms of the sorts of people working on both sides of the trade.

These similarities should not be more than a minor digression from the main discussion – but if you are waiting for the coffee to arrive, sometimes this 'warm-up ' part of the meeting is profitably spent establishing some common ground.

REMIND THEM OF PEOPLE IN COMMON

Although interests and experiences in common are helpful, relationships are more powerful as ways of building rapport because of the emotional element. When two people both know the same person, even if their perceptions are very different, they have a bond because this person is in their network of friends or colleagues.

'How do you know Peter [the intermediary to the meeting]?' is a question which either you or the client might reasonably ask and it will lead to a different sort of conversation from a comment about having the same model of laptop. We are naturally curious about the other's experience of the person we know and we each recognize that there is a chance that either party will be reporting back to Peter about the meeting. We also wonder how far the other person *really* knows Peter, or whether Peter is simply fulfilling some obligation to a person he hardly knows. A conversation about a third person is therefore more intimate and ultimately revealing than a conversation about public transport chaos mutually experienced on the way to work.

The topic of Peter automatically leads to a different sort of personal introduction. 'So, did Peter tell you anything about me or what we do... or...?' If the answer is negative, you can introduce yourself, but generally the introductory email will have provided you with some hooks about the client you can build on. If Peter has phoned the new client – or the client has checked you out by phoning him – then you can fill in the gaps. Then you reciprocate. 'Unfortunately, he was a lot less forthcoming about you! To be fair, I haven't been able to reach him as he has been travelling for the last couple of weeks, so ... please, tell me a bit about how you come to be in the job.' Such an invitation to the client to tell you their life story would not be possible without the preceding conversation about Peter.

REFLECT COMMON VALUES

The most powerful bond between people is their values. Research into long-term relationships show that, although many personality traits do not indicate the propensity for the relationship to endure, openness – to ideas, aesthetics, actions and values – does. When we find others who feel the same way about an issue as we do, who share our values, we make a stronger connection than if we have only experiences or relationships in common.

It can work both ways. Clients who have values that are very different from our own are often the hardest to work with. We often intuit this before we recognize what the source of our unease is about. Sometimes it is the chance remark that lets us know that this person sees the world in a very different way. 'Nobody really believes that, do they...?' 'People like that should be taken out and shot...' 'Women tend to...' This means we will have to work harder to find the common ground.

The simple way appears to be to agree with what the client expresses, and taking the line of least resistance works... up to a point. Saying nothing to raise the issue of your values being different from the client's certainly makes sense in early meetings. But, as you will have to continue as you start, it would be better to find areas where you generally share attitudes or beliefs, rather than pretend. Agreeing to disagree is a sign of a mature relationship and is probably a better goal for a trusted salesperson than passive acceptance of the client's values.

Putting it all together

Relationships grow where similarities are discovered; these can be experiences, relationships or, most powerfully, shared values. On first meeting a client, you not only need to assess them in terms of their value as a prospect, but also find the common ground.

23 GIFTS CREATE OBLIGATIONS

'It is amazing what you can accomplish if you do not care who gets the credit.'

Harry Truman

If you want to be trusted, you need to think about how trusted advisers sell. What are clients' assumptions about advisers compared to salespeople? First, they assume that advisers are better informed. They read specialist journals, attend conferences, have academic qualifications or publications relevant to their areas of interest. They are up to date on what is happening in different sectors. They have specialist knowledge in adjacent technical areas. Secondly, they are reliable – dull compared to salespeople. Thirdly, they are passionate about what they do and they love solving problems.

Some of these assumptions need to inform how you behave at early meetings:

- You will want to know whether your knowledge can help the client.
- You will be curious about the client's situation.
- You will not feel you have to demonstrate your expertise in any way, except in response to the client.
- You will transparently want to help rather than sell.
- You will willingly share ideas and information, giving things away in every sentence.

The first meetings with the lead can establish your positioning as an adviser in the client's eyes. Of course, you will be smartly dressed, but what car will you drive? Top salespeople drive nice cars, but top advisers, aware of not seeming to be too insensitive, choose a form of transport appropriate to their client's status rather than reinforcing their own. Partners in PWC used to make consultants all travel in the same Ford fleet car to visit clients in local government, and saved the BMWs for visiting the bankers.

What you take as a 'thank you' to the lead is important. If you bring something that is professionally laid out with sensible content and some interesting conclusions (which can be discussed), you will immediately confront the client's low expectations of salespeople and raise the value perception of your brand. If you focus your gift specifically on their company situation, this will be even more impressive. Most impressive of all is something that focuses not just on their industry but something they can use themselves to look good with their team or boss. (The aim is to engage other stakeholders, so make it easy for the lead.)

FOCUS YOUR 'GIFT' ON WHAT MATTERS TO THEM, NOT YOU

Creating a gift that will make the meeting worth the time the client has given you is a tough challenge. Unless you are a sole trader or a small business, this is unlikely to be all your own work – others will have made a contribution. (The second meeting may involve some of them coming to see other clients.) In B2B this is the initial currency of trade – the barter of information, which you give clients in exchange for the information they give you.

Advisers with only an hour would prepare five slides, each of which has a slightly provocative conclusion as its headline about a topic, any of which will interest the target. One successful salesperson – who never takes anything on paper to the first meeting, but always follows up with a written document and a personal note – said, 'You need to provide them with ammunition with which to impress their boss.' This means that, if they are operational managers, you need to provide conclusions about policy and tactics. If they are middle managers, you need to provide conclusions about metrics, results and structure. Senior managers – who will be sharing ideas with their colleagues – need conclusions about strategy, market trends, technological shifts, regulation and shareholder value.

The conclusions are always about opportunity. Change starts with a gentle nudge to the complacency you find in all organizations. Many B2B sales are about change. People have to realize that either things will not always continue in the same (positive) way or that they have a chance to move ahead more quickly or profitably than they ever imagined. This is warming them up to the possibility of improvement, not showing them a vision of what better will look like, nor how your solution will help to get them there – that will come later.

Furthermore

Never, ever carry marketing material about your company, your products or your CV. This is what clients expect from sales reps, order takers and job applicants. If they are interested, your website should answer those sorts of questions and they will probably already have looked you and your company up – just as you have researched them.

STIMULATE DEBATE ABOUT FUTURE OPPORTUNITIES, NOT PAST FAILURE

Most sales organizations produce brochures or generic reports as marketing collateral. Although this is interesting in a general way, it is less engaging for clients than something more focused on their own situation. (If the research has been given press coverage, such as a commentary on regulation by your CE, sometimes the desire to be 'part of the story' may also get you talking.) Ideally, therefore, you should write the document after you have met the client rather than before. But you may also feel that you have promised something that you need to deliver on, so you are rather caught in a dilemma.

Do you show *general* ideas and conclusions before and risk their rejection? Can you show *specific* conclusions about your client's situation and issues afterwards? Here, the approach used by professional advisers may be instructive. They work on the principle that, before they undertake to address a new market or geography, they must establish their credibility with analysis (which can be sponsored, independent analysis produced by a business school, for example). They will also always follow up with specific conclusions to their client, based on what they have been told. The MAC group – the erstwhile strategy department of Cap Gemini – used to return from a briefing with a client and aim to have faxed through ten hand-drawn slides within a couple of hours to their client's desk. This looked like the work of the consultants who had met the lead, but actually was the result of a group of analysts who started work as soon as they were briefed over the phone by the consultants leaving the client. The idea of 'hand drawn' was to personalize and demonstrate that this was initial thinking, not final draft.

Whatever the decision about content and its timing, it is important that what you present is an argument rather than just information. A business case 'argument' means that, when you state a problem or opportunity in your slide headline, you support it with facts and figures on the body of the slide. If the individual slides don't hang together as a 'story' (a problem in final pitches), it doesn't matter at this point; you are presenting conclusions to provoke discussion. Some people write their conclusions as questions to assist in the process of engaging the client, forcing them to engage with the analysis.

DON'T THINK LIKE A SALESPERSON BEFORE YOU SPOT THE *REAL* OPPORTUNITY

Product world salespeople are hard-wired to want to close as soon as they can. They imagine that the client will lose interest if they don't and never come back. Close too early and you may miss the real opportunity – the higher-value deal.

Your gift is to start the process of opening up the client and her organization. Your aim is to create a good impression of your company's capabilities, not through talking about them but by demonstrating them in the way you work with the lead on the topic. Your assumption is that, even if they tell you what they want, it may not be what they need (which is what they will ultimately value). You do not yet understand the scope of the opportunity, the decision-making process and, more importantly, the client doesn't understand the true value of a solution. 'If the fix is too quick, it must be easy and cheap', as one salesperson expressed it.

So your gift is all about discussion, expanding the universe of possibility for the client, and not about certainty and closure. If the gift works, it helps you to:

- get more meetings and more discussions
- introduce more of your competent people to other leads
- get permission to do some exploratory work on the dimensions of the issue for the client.

Any of these outcomes might be sparked by the conversation around the topic your conclusions provoke.

Accept that, with B2B solutions selling, at the start it is often genuinely ambiguous. Keeping it vague, encouraging your client to let it stay vague a while longer, reassuring your client that uncertainty is not just inevitable but it can also be creative and productive... these are the ways you should be thinking. If you initiated the call, the client probably hasn't completely diagnosed any problems and neither have you. If they called you in, perhaps thinking about putting together an RFP, they will appreciate your expanding their thinking. If you label the opportunity too soon – which is what salespeople are sometimes trained to do – you may miss the much bigger opportunity around the corner.

Although the cliché about this use of marketing bait is 'the sprat to catch the mackerel', I prefer to think of your gift as being the key that opens the tin of sardines.

Putting it all together

Giving clients ideas, information and analysis that they find valuable creates a sense of obligation. Professional advisers sell using these gifts as ways to open up the discussion of what the client needs and values, on the assumption that this isn't clear to *either* party at the start of the meeting.

If the client can define their requirement, they commoditize what you offer. They in effect standardize what you would like to customize. Avoid the tendency to close on even what seems to be a clear-cut order by probing the outcomes the client really wants.

24 WORKING SESSIONS, NOT PITCHES

'To own is to have. To have is to hold. To hold is to show off.'
Don Rushkoff

Firstly, there's the technology to overcome:

'We were pitching to the board of one of the clearing banks. You never remember the project, you always remember the situation – which I guess is how most clients feel. Anyway, the suits were out in force, grim-faced, as well they might be; we were the third firm to pitch. We had pulled it together last minute and the technology of the time – the overhead projector – required you to print up slides on flimsy sheets of acetate, secured in a cardboard frame. Except we hadn't had time to frame them. The partner did the usual insincere words of thanks for the opportunity, made the introductions and we were off.

'I was the slide jockey and the "subject matter expert" on the project, required to support the partner whenever he confronted a question he wasn't sure of, which, to be fair, was rare. On goes the first slide. The projector is boiling hot despite the whirring fan and the acetate film curls up like a cat in front of the fire. Roger spotted the problem immediately and, pro that he was, indicated to me to get down on my knees and to hold the slide in place. On the other side of the projector he did the same, and we delivered the pitch like supplicants at court. We won. Maybe that's the lesson: begging pays...'

The promoters of presentation technology have been saying for years that what people see they remember. (The bankers probably remembered the begging.) It is also true that what people see they do not necessarily absorb. Another partner in a professional services firm expressed the view that PowerPoint was good for getting compliance – 'No more slides! Please! We agree!' – and for controlling complicated groups of stakeholders, but lousy for stimulating discussion and commitment. A client who said yes after a long presentation often changed their mind.

The reason is not far to seek: presenting salespeople are expecting too much of their audience. The gathering of clients must:

- understand the concept
- accept the reasons why it is correct both rationally and emotionally (change is a very emotive subject)
- reach some sort of consensus – whether compliant with the group leader or truly committed.

– and all in less than an hour. That's quite a tall order when there are alternatives.

STIMULATE INTERACTION IF YOU WANT AGREEMENT

Writing the proposal before the meeting and distributing it to all the participants beforehand helps to overcome the 'understanding' aspect of the process. Reading requires effort but is generally the best way for people to absorb information and prepare themselves for sensible discussion.

This might not be your first choice. Many salespeople I have met prefer to focus on their performance on stage more than their performance on the page. But both are important, if you set out to stimulate interaction. And the performance is less Henry V, and more about asking questions and letting the clients do more of the talking – that is, if your ego can take it.

You will still need a presentation but only a short one, which highlights the main point in the pre-read document, perhaps ten slides including the agenda. What you will need to do is prepare the process of the meeting with some degree of rehearsal. Experienced salespeople hate rehearsing because they are good presenters and like the adrenalin rush of thinking on their feet.

But many experienced salespeople do rehearse:

> 'So gentlemen, we have come here this morning in the expectation that you have read our proposals, and to convince you that this is the right way to proceed and we are the best people to proceed with. On first reading, how are we doing?'

The tone, note, is respectful ('gentlemen') but confident ('how are we doing?'). My interviewee says that there is usually a bit of a silence, as they are used to presenters who allow them to sleep through the first slides and wake up only when the detail appears on the screen.

The audience either declare themselves – 'Er... didn't read it', 'Have quite a few questions about the costs', 'Liked the basic idea' – or say nothing. When they have all said something and he has established that this won't just be a formal presentation, he follows this up with:

> 'We want today's session to be a discussion because we sincerely believe that change, of the sort we have all been discussing over the last months, only really happens when those responsible for leading it – you – are really aligned about the objectives and the approach. So here is our draft agenda for today. What's missing for anybody here?'

He shows the slide.

There is a well-established sales technique called 'get them saying yes'. You ask a lot of fairly obvious questions of your audience to get them nodding or agreeing. The idea is that this pattern of agreement to agendas and coffee breaks carries over to the more complex sort of agreement about a large sum of money. My interviewee thought this simplistic approach was nonsense and patronizing. His intention was to engage them in decision-making rather than simply agreeing, and when somebody wanted something in the agenda changed he saw this as progress; the group were starting to see that they needed consensus and that he and the team were the means to get to this.

He then sets up the 'rules of engagement' which his company expects at this point. All conversations are in confidence and nobody will report on this outside the group without the group's agreement. No right or wrong answers; this meeting is about seeking ideas and ultimately consensus, and this takes time. The proposal they have read remains a draft until that point.

WORK 'WITH' RATHER THAN WORK 'FOR'

Pitching is often synonymous with 'pleasing'. The presenter attempts to make the proposal and the team as desirable as possible, but, if what the client really values is unclear, the default to 'being nice' can be bland.

'Nice' is not necessarily valuable – 'energetic', 'committed', 'confident', 'stimulating' or even 'conflictual' might also be worth having, if the sponsoring client's diagnosis is that their organization is complacent or in denial about the need for change. Salespeople rarely ask their potential sponsor 'How would you like us to play the presentation tomorrow?' but maybe they should at least ask, because this demonstrates that the pitching company is on an equal footing with their client and not subservient. The client may be reluctant to advise but this doesn't make the question redundant.

In the product world the customer is always right, but with solutions neither the buyer nor the seller can be entirely right at this point in the game. The adult position is to agree and disagree with your client when in a working session, but never to make your client feel bad when you have to disagree. In effect, you say, 'We are both making history here. We must continue to talk. We will give this 120 per cent. But you are our client and ultimately you call the shots, unless we really feel that you are making a big mistake when we are obliged to tell you so, based on our expertise and experience.'

Confidence therefore means:

- dialogue, not didacticism
- demonstrating, not describing
- the association of equals with complementary knowledge and experience, through a contract.

Consider your last pitch. How far did you communicate this sort of confidence?

LET THE CUSTOMER 'HANDLE THE GOODS'

A common retail customer question is 'So do you drive/eat/use this yourself?' What the customer is interested in is a personal experience of the product, because handling the goods supports three different functions in the buying process:

1. It communicates the seller's confidence in what the product can do.
2. It reinforces the feeling of ownership.
3. It allows the salesperson to encourage comparisons between the product in the customer's hands with what he has at home already, the competitor's product, or the one he saw the day before.

The pitch-as-working-session is the client's chance to 'handle the goods'. In solutions terms, this means discovering the solution-in-use. When the solution is a replacement purchase or a renewal, this 'test' is also a good moment to ask questions of comparison around features or benefits, if you are sure that the solution they are trying outperforms their existing solution. Emphasizing benefits in a generic way is never as effective as highlighting a benefit you know the client values, where the potential purchase outperforms the current option. 'How much flexibility on storage do you get in your current system?' (Questions like this work only when your solution is better than their current system *and* flexible storage is a benefit they really value. Unless both are the case, your solution's superior performance is irrelevant.)

Naturally, there are some risks to customers 'handling the goods' in this way. They may end up gathering information that *discourages* them from buying. There can be negative as well as positive points of comparison. Faulty performance in the room has to be managed; a system which won't boot up, a screen link which fails to work, even a data projector malfunction (not your fault) can have a negative impact on the audience. Rehearse these elements, just as you would consider the impact of a power cut on your team's performance. (Would you? Working in some parts of the world, you should.)

Putting it all together

Pitching is a performance where your audience remains mostly passive. Decision-making is, however, a process that needs active discussion and ultimately commitment to act differently as a company.

Many early-stage pitches would be better run as working sessions. Salespeople are ambivalent about letting clients discuss things endlessly. They feel that they must close and move on, and final pitches/beauty parades may indeed be about this process when you are down to the last two. Stimulating engagement with discussion and demonstration is more work, but it provides experience of how your company will serve this client, which is usually a critical part of any client's decision.

25 THE MATRIX MARCHES TO YOUR TUNE

'He who pays the piper calls the tune.'

Proverb

What do most clients worry most about when they contemplate a big solution like outsourcing? It's joined-up delivery. They know, often from their own experience, that complex operations are a headache to run: customer-unresponsive, inflexible, problematic in terms of knowing who is really going to carry the can when things go wrong, and full of issues around quality, completeness and timeliness. From your side, you know that, if you don't get this about 99 per cent right in the first week, there will be long-term relationship issues to deal with.

Often, it is the functional separation of sales from delivery that produces this problem. One salesperson expressed it like this:

> 'When I first started I couldn't even get the specialists to give me the technical details I needed for the proposal – a basic response to an RFP. They were grumpy and seemed to resent the fact that our efforts created their job security. They complained more than clients and muttered about us over-selling, just as we used to complain about them under-delivering.'

This 'us' and 'them' division isn't just about sales and the rest; it happens in many parts of large organizations.

Enter the delivery manager. Every salesperson needs a close working relationship with several positive service delivery managers with whom to work on bids. Delivery or project managers tend to be a dry, laconic crowd, calm in the eye of the hurricane and rightly proud of their ability to pull miracles out of nothing. To be able to show the closeness of that working relationship between yourself and the delivery team to a new client is possibly the most reassuring sight of all. Well-rehearsed group pitches, cheerful working relationships demonstrated at prospecting meetings, your ability to get a rapid response from a specialist in your organization – all these will be observed and noted by the client as part of their risk-management strategy.

INVOLVE THE DELIVERY MANAGEMENT TEAM IN THE SALE

Professional services firms have to involve the delivery experts as clients expect to meet their legal or audit team as part of the process of deciding. When they appear, the hierarchy of command is clear: the partner with reliable judgement based on experience; the manager, eager and ambitious, keen to make a good impression; and the juniors with pale faces from working long hours, but sharp as ice picks. And everybody is dressed as though they could jump on the plane for their client right now...

As solutions become more tailored, so the relationship with the tailor may become more important. If he is in Bangalore, the client may still expect to see him because of the issue of responsiveness. A human relationship is often more important than a service-level agreement, the existence of which speaks volumes about both parties' expectations on goodwill. A brilliant team, for which the client will pay over the odds, can be as important as the savings spreadsheet in their perception of value and risk.

One excellent salesperson likened this to choosing a cardiologist, which he had once had to do:

'I saw six, all in Harley Street [London's premier street for private medical practices], but the gulf between the best and worst was enormous. The best explained things really well. He really listened. He was genuinely interested in his work. He was happy for his team to talk, the anaesthetist and so on. He wanted to bring me along with the whole thing. I don't know if he was technically the best – how could I tell? – but that was when I made up my mind.

I think it is much the same with complex sales. Clients can't discriminate in terms of technical elements, the solutions are too complicated technically or organizationally. But they can decide what sort of delivery team they trust...'

SHARE CLIENT EXPECTATION MANAGEMENT

Most clients will have encountered disappointing performance in services they have bought. When the service is complex and mediated by software they don't fully understand, they probably expect to be disappointed again, even though they are paying a lot of money. So they expect to complain, and set up systems that enable them to track promised outcomes and timings.

When customers have little idea about how the solution will really benefit them, they focus on what they do know – the cost and time aspects of your proposal. They often push hardest on things like how long a particular function takes, costs per transaction and why you can't start work immediately.

This suggests that 'strategic concept' – sales-speak for high-level benefits – is not that important. As with the delivery team, as the sale progresses the customer will increasingly focus on the concrete, observable elements of what they are buying. They might get extremely excited about throughput rates, output quality and deadlines. Because these are the only aspect of the solution which the client understands – and feels they should control – they will often make the definition of this aspect of the solution a key part of the service-level agreement and insist on features like reimbursement for late delivery. It's not about fancy words on PowerPoint, but just good, reliable delivery management.

The reality is that trade-offs between time, cost and quality are inevitable in all services (as are trade-offs between the satisfaction levels of different stakeholders). As the salesperson, you are not always in the best position to judge what is the most appropriate balance to these things, whereas the delivery team can quote examples of the impact of making poor trade-offs. When the prospect is contemplating the options or even a chosen option, this is often the point at which to include delivery specialists in the discussion; their experience – superior to that of both the salesperson and the client – can often manage client expectations to result in a better solution all round.

Your ability to produce the right people from your organization to address these detailed questions of performance is often vital. As one solutions client expressed it:

'Of course, the salesperson will tell you that it can be done – that's their job, to get you excited by the possibility. But I want to hear this promise from the lips of the person who has actually delivered this before. I want to know his views and I want to know what goes wrong and how he will deal with it. If he and the salesperson are broadly in agreement, I trust both of them more.'

GIVE YOURSELF THE TASK OF QUALITY ASSURANCE

You are making a promise on behalf of your company, so it seems logical to the client that you should be responsible for delivering that promise.

This might only require you to meet the sponsors once a quarter, perhaps take them out to lunch and check on progress of delivery. Well briefed by the delivery manager, these meetings not only confirm your commitment to helping them improve their business but also uncover other sales opportunities: unforeseen problems which the new system is revealing; the need to change the specification to respond to a nimble competitor; the difficulty that some users are having adapting to the new approach. Of course, this is only a viable role if you clearly have some 'clout' over the process of delivery – a proxy for client interests with your own organization.

The quality-assurance role also helps to identify new opportunities. What start out as progress reviews may provide you with evidence for outcomes delivered (and intelligence about where the solution has not performed as expected). The meetings can also build relationships with clients. The ability to help is often missed because the salesperson is spending too much time trying to find new clients, when they could simply be building on existing client relationships to either unearth new opportunities or get introductions. Maintaining an ongoing dialogue with your best customers is often the best way to meet quota, if they have budget.

A story from an ex-salesman in oil industry software illustrates this. His product was used to predict the progress of oil spills at sea and was in wide use around the world. On a trip to Java he found himself with a free afternoon and decided to look for oil companies in Yellow Pages. He rang up a potential lead and explained what his product did. 'What a pity,' said the manager, 'we have just given this contract to somebody else. But why not come over anyway and maybe you can help me with something else.' This chance meeting turned into several millions of sales over the following years. Serendipity – the chance discovery of something valuable while looking for something else – is nurtured by taking on the role of ensuring the quality of the delivery with the project manager.

Putting it all together

Clients are sceptical of sales promises about solutions, so involving delivery managers and technical people in the formulation and communication of those promises helps to demonstrate that you can deliver what you promise. You are the conductor of an orchestra over which you have limited authority. And your client is watching to see how you cope.

One way to do this is to give yourself the ongoing role of assuring the quality of the delivery. This is not usually the case in technical businesses, although it is usually the role of the partner in professional services. It allows for regular meetings with the client and thus the tracking of benefits (useful for future sales) and the uncovering of unmet needs (ditto).

26 NOT EVERY CLIENT IS A GOOD CLIENT

'Success is 99 per cent failure.'
Sochira Honda

What do you make of the point of view expressed in this remark? Is it inevitable that you will fail more often than you succeed? For most product salespeople, the rejection and the unanswered call are just part of the job and they comfort themselves with the idea that their timing wasn't right or that each rejection means they are one step closer to success – both of which are numerically true but not emotionally satisfying enough for many people who are not in sales. All that 'failure' – if this is the correct word, which I doubt – reinforces the sense that selling is transactional rather than genuinely relational. It may engender cynicism about customers or the whole process of selling.

Successful salespeople, you would imagine, have a much higher average success rate than others, and when you talk with them they may initially claim that this is so. They are also much more tactical than the average salesperson in the clients they choose to invest in, which means their averages *look* better. Experience has shown them that the 80/20 rule applies to selling, as in many endeavours; the challenge is to pick the 20 per cent of clients who will make your numbers.

There is no easy formula. You need a lot of intuition about people and their needs, which experience sharpens, but there are some simple questions you can ask yourself about the client in front of you which may help in any client selection process:

- Does this person have the sort of budget our service needs? Will this person ever be in a position to pay our sort of invoices?

- Do I find this person easy to do business with? Do they share the same values as me? Is there an easy rapport?
- Is this person motivated by the same things our service/ solution provides? Do they feel that the outcomes we can ensure are valuable enough?
- Are our two companies complementary? Is our intellectual know-how complementary? Will we both be stronger together than apart?
- Is this person attracted to changing things for the better or is their motivation to conserve what they have?

CONSIDER WHAT MOTIVATIONAL PATTERNS YOUR SOLUTION IS LIKELY TO APPEAL TO

Clients are motivated differently at different stages in their working lives and by the business environment in which they find themselves. While the need for services that reduce costs and increase efficiencies (or which maximize growth and return on investment) are in part a reflection of the wider economy and the performance of their business, individual motivations are also important to understand when considering the longer-term value of a client relationship. If your service is about efficiency, then clients who are motivated by structure and money will make better customers regardless of their company's performance.

You can do this by reviewing successful and unsuccessful sales experiences. When customers buy, ask yourself which aspects of your solution appeal to them? What sort of customer shows no interest? Why? Circumstances when the customer *should* be interested but isn't – or the reverse – are often the most illuminating.

A very successful salesperson who sells leadership training described a visit to a new client:

'I went to the client thinking that they wouldn't really be interested in training. They weren't doing well and had been hit hard by the recession, and in my line of work your experience indicates that the first thing to get cut is training. You always hope to meet the internal customer of training and not the training department, because then there is more hope of a sale, and we did; we had been recommended to the operations director by another client. So we started the meeting with the usual conversation about the performance of the business (dire) and how people were reacting (depression) and what they had been doing to combat this and keep people going (not much). The guy knew we provided leadership development, so I said something about recession being a crisis for management but an opportunity for leadership. "I agree 100 per cent," he said. "The board has agreed a substantial budget for this work which we have never had before." "With what exactly in mind?" I asked, trying to hide my surprise. "Nothing concrete. Not yet. They don't understand it. I'm just committed to doing this for the company and I've persuaded them.""

The client strongly valued leadership development, based on powerful personal experience, and was looking for partners.

Professor John Hunt of London Business School created a model of motivational factors that suggests that people are driven differently at different stages in their lives and that, to some extent, motivation is influenced by culture and gender. Although the details of these patterns are not important, having an idea of what sort of motivations your solution appeals to is, when deciding on the longer-term value of a client to invest in. Hunt's list of motivators includes money to spend, avoidance of risk, structure, recognition, managerial power, team affiliation, avoidance of working alone, creativity and autonomy. If your solution supports the idea of enhanced structure and team affiliation, knowing that these things matter to your client too will make a longer-term sales relationship more likely.

You can guess client motivations from their behaviour and how they organize their environment. We all know that a client with an array of certificates on the wall probably wants recognition and you will try hard to make this sort of client look good. But considering also whether your solution provides this benefit is what we are talking about here; if, say, your leadership training enables the person to be seen as an exemplar of leadership, you may find the idea easier to sell to this client.

Outcomes that appeal to those motivated by money to spend would, of course, include cost reduction. Risk avoiders like solutions that guarantee processes that are currently uncertain. Teambuilding appeals more to those who are themselves motivated by their affiliation to a team... and so on. Considering your solution in these terms may give you better ideas about how to discriminate more between the clients you meet.

INVEST MORE IN THOSE OPEN TO CHANGE AND WHO SEE YOU AS AN ALLY

Complex solutions are disruptive, so change aversion is not a good motivator in general, for customers of solution providers. Courage is required and this is often absent in clients with large mortgages to pay, who, let us imagine, work in a large insurance firm in the City of London. Everybody loves the idea of leading a major change but many fear the consequences of failure too much.

Salespeople use a number of techniques to de-risk change for their clients, but the reality is that brave or foolhardy clients are easier to work with in this respect. They will expect you to be equally fearless, of course, and to back them to the hilt, but in general they are worth the ride in the longer term as such clients are loyal to their people, and you become one of 'their people'. They will also be demanding because they want 400 per cent of anything you offer.

If they have the appetite but lack the skill – particularly in handling politics – they may be mavericks rather than good leaders. This reputation will make them less influential in the organization, so look for people who are both keen and skilful.

PULL BACK ON THE TIME YOU INVEST IN THE REST

Prioritizing relationship time is important, if you are to give of your best to the best of your clients. There are clients who will waste your time; they have no budget readily available – and no strong likelihood of getting one – but they like to talk about ideas and be given information.

'The clients who seem to be on endless fishing trips are sometimes hard to deal with, especially if they are senior. I have a rule about reciprocation; if they want analysis or information from me, I ask for a similar piece of work from them. If they want introductions to other clients, I ask for the same.'

If the relationship is going to be valuable without any immediate prospect of a sale, you need to check that the clients are also prepared to invest. If they aren't, you are best advised to look elsewhere, no matter how senior they are.

Putting it all together

Don't give equal effort to all clients. Think about which ones will help you to achieve your target, principally this year but also in years to come. Manage your diary to check that you are investing in the relationships you value, as well as the deals.

Research into customer loyalty by Dixon and Adamson showed that it was driven most (53 per cent) by 'the purchase experience' – what the clients experienced during the sales cycle. Less influential were company brand (19 per cent), service delivery record (19 per cent) and value-to-price ratio (9 per cent). The 'purchase experience' included providing perspectives on the market, the creation of alternatives, how easy the supplier was to buy from (e.g. no legal delays) and how widespread the support for the supplier was in the organization. Once you have chosen your clients, it is worth investing in their experience of buying from you.

27 PRESSURIZING CLIENTS CAN COST YOU THE DEAL

'If it be now, 'tis not to come. If it be not to come, it will be now. If it be not now, yet it will come – the readiness is all.'
William Shakespeare, Hamlet

There's always a bit of pressure in selling. The quarter's end looms nearer, you seem close to achieving your target, only for it to recede, and the boss gives you that look at the monthly sales meeting. You turn that pressure into exerting pressure on the client.

Think of it the other way around. If you were the customer and the salesperson said, 'No... take your time. Think about it. Think about it some more. We can start whenever you feel the time is right for you', how would you feel? How about if the salesperson said, 'Let me know when you want a proposal from us.' What would you think about the company they represented? You might think they had lousy salespeople, if your company culture is hard driving, transactional about relationships and extremely competitive. You might also think they must be doing really well to be so chilled about closing the deal; perhaps they are really busy?

Timing when to propose can materially affect your chances of success. Many things influence client readiness for a proposal, including:

- budget cycles
- the short-term availability of cash
- the desire to finish the job of scoping the project and find out what and how you will charge

- their need to show something to other people in the company
- the timetable they agreed with their boss and procurement.

These reasons are what should drive your timetable, not your own need to secure the sale in quarter three.

Writing a really good proposal takes a lot of time because of the complex commitments you are making. Pushing your client works well when it comes to offering help or if there is a crisis, but is not so good when it comes to managing the proposal deadline. A proposal is a sort of ultimatum, and if you time it badly the client may dodge the issue by saying no.

IDENTIFY WHAT IS DRIVING ANY DECISION-MAKING TIMETABLE ON THE CLIENT SIDE

Just as you are subject to targets linked to some timetable, so will your clients be. But the corporate timetable doesn't mean the client is ready to buy from *you*. There is the official version of 'readiness' – all processes duly carried out – and there is the more personal version, too. Quite often, it is the sponsor's decision-making style that determines the pace at which choices and final decisions can be made.

Clients vary widely in the deliberation and patience with which they approach decisions. More active and impulsive types prefer to move fast and, if the corporate will is to move slowly, they may rely on trusted members of their circle to do the due diligence. When this has been done and you are down to the final three or four, they make a rapid decision at the beauty parade of competing bidders. At the other end of the scale are clients who want not only to pore over the details of the proposal but also to cross-examine you on these finer points. You may have been in meetings where both sorts of client decision-maker are represented; the frustration on both sides can seep out.

Spotting these sorts of differences is hard to do without first-hand experience of the person. Academics Gary Williams and Robert Miller suggested that there were five decision-making styles, which persuaders should respond to:

1. **Followers** (36 per cent of executives) – who, as late adopters, like proof of past success
2. **Charismatics** (25 per cent) – who are mostly focused on results
3. **Thinkers** (11 per cent) – the logical, detail-oriented types who follow their heads
4. **Sceptics** (19 per cent) – who like to challenge but ultimately decide with their gut
5. **Controllers** (9 per cent) – whose hatred of uncertainty means they prefer their own ideas to yours.

Their decision-making preferences also influenced their ideal timetable for making the decision:

- **Followers** are influenced by brand and track record. You need to enhance their confidence with proven methods and results. They will move at the pace of the peer group or in the way the company usually makes decisions of this sort.
- **Charismatics** want to move quickly from the big idea to the details of implementation. They know their enthusiasm can get them into hot water, so they want evidence of results. They are rapid decision-makers.
- **Thinkers** want as much information as they can. As they dislike risk and are not impressed by charm, they need intelligent, factual answers. They will take their time.
- **Sceptics** are big personalities and you know where you stand with them. Credibility must be earned, including in the way you respond to their challenges; assume they know the stuff already rather than try to teach them. They are quick decision-makers.
- **Controllers** think they are the best at everything – including buying and selling. They see things only from their own perspective. They hate to be rushed.

DON'T BE PUSHED INTO PROPOSING TOO EARLY

Clients like to set impossible deadlines for proposals the first time you sell to them. This may be an unconscious or a conscious way of testing your company's commitment and reliability. When they know that you deliver, they are often open to a more flexible approach to delivering a proposal, depending on the degree of urgency they see in the situation.

Salespeople generally like to respond to the schedule the client prefers. If anything, they prefer a sale to be moving forward rapidly, as this may reduce competition and much of the sales team effort goes into performing extraordinary feats in double-quick time. This confirms the self-perception of many salespeople as gallant miracle workers. But is this assumption correct? Which would you value more: the instant gratification of the coffee out of the machine or the delayed gratification of the artisan coffee shop where the beans are selected, freshly ground and filtered? A small delay actually helps the client to value the work that has gone into the proposal itself, which may give you some advantage in competitive situations.

If you can deliver only a poor proposal because the client imposes an overly tight timetable on the team, consider negotiating. As everywhere in the sales process, behaving like the client's business partner – a relationship of mutual respect – means that stating your needs and expectations is allowed. They can always say no and that tells you something, too. Is it a 'make-weight' proposal to aid negotiation rather than a serious attempt to get the best result, perhaps?

FIND OUT HOW THE CLIENT FEELS ABOUT THE PROCESS BEFORE DECIDING ON YOUR TACTICS

Timing is part of managing expectations. Usually, the proposal-writing process signals the end of dialogue and the start of the vendor(s) having to reveal their hand in exchange for whatever information the customer has provided. This is only custom and practice and, unless there is a procurement rule forbidding this, you should continue to talk with your clients right up to the beauty parade:

- Share a draft proposal – incomplete – for feedback.
- Share information relevant to their need – academic articles, research findings or news – and elicit a response.

- Agree the structure of the proposal before showing the sponsor the content.
- Give the sponsor a first sight of any document before it is shared with other stakeholders. Before the beauty parade your strongest sponsor needs to know what you are going to say; they may even offer you public support as a result.

This 'preview' overcomes some of the difficulties of timing, too. You can send the more eager and thoughtful 'draft' before the final deadline and have a brief feedback session over the phone, which may help you to sharpen up key points. Any preview should also prevent you from saying anything unwittingly defamatory or inflammatory.

As the deadline approaches, the client's sunk costs increase; the time they are spending on the deal means that they are less likely to take the loss and just walk away.

Putting it all together

How you behave with regard to time indicates your commitment to the client. Different clients prefer to make their decisions to different timetables and an RFP process reveals a lot about the organization's approach to managing time.

Time, cost and quality tend to be in opposition to one another when it comes to proposals (as with service delivery), so be clear to spell out any consequences for the client of a too-hurried proposal. The 'right' time is what is right for both parties to do the best job and produce the best decision.

28 PROPOSALS ANSWER CLIENT QUESTIONS

'In choosing a supplier... customers know the important questions to ask. Is the supplier credible? Do I trust the salesperson? Does the product function adequately? Is it materially better than my in-house options? How competitive is the price? Is the product reliable? Are the warranty and service offers acceptable? What are the financing options? Can we/ they get it installed and running? Will it work with other stuff we already bought?'
Wood, Hewlin and Lah

Proposals are often dull, following a structure either imposed by the RFP or the standards of the competing firms. Reading them is like marking exam scripts; you dutifully check to see that they have mentioned all the salient points, but only occasionally does one really stand out.

This is because the proposal is a draft contractual document as well as a sales pitch. It's hard to pull off such a combination. Successful salespeople reckon that a proposal hardly ever 'wins' you the deal, and that time spent on crafting and redrafting a document or presentation would be better spent face to face with the sponsors and stakeholders – if they will let you. High-quality face time is a better predictor of success than deathless prose or lively PowerPoint. In other words, separating the two elements – exciting them with ideas and reassuring them about capability and contractual detail, including price – might be better done in separate documents.

B2B proposals contain a common list of contractual elements:

1. The context of the need – this is often a change in the business environment that has triggered the need for guidance, new

technology, professional service, outsourcing or whatever. This element establishes 'We understand', which is necessary for the client to read more.

2. The client's desired outcome(s) – beneficial changes to their business that will be valuable to the company in specified ways (e.g. increased efficiency, higher revenues, lower costs). This element sets out what has been agreed between sponsors and stakeholders about the scope of the solution or project. This is what you are promising to deliver.

3. The providing company's approach to helping – this might specify the type of solution, the way you will solve the problem, perhaps how your company thinks about such issues and helps clients deal with them. This section also covers what benefits the client can expect from the solution.

4. The qualifications of the providing company to assist – these might be anything from detailed case studies to a list of references. This is to establish your competence. Some clients never read this part as they reckon you will have been vetted for basic competence by Procurement or the sponsor.

5. The people involved and how they will communicate. The definition of the 'team' and the structure around the delivery process varies widely; for professional services, names and CVs are normal; for more technical solutions, often only the more senior managers are named on both the client and provider side. This confirms who will be responsible for what.

6. The timetable for designing and introducing the solution – this manages expectations about what will be delivered and when.

7. Costs – fees, expenses and how payments will be made. Some proposals separate out this element into a separate document, as different people handle price negotiations and payment terms. It also enables you to get agreement on scope before you discuss costs. This deals with the commercial aspects.

8. Legal/risk management. This section anticipates risks to the preceding promises of benefits and proposes ways to handle them.

9. Supporting evidence. As proposals can run to many pages, often details of the content appear as appendices: for example your terms and conditions of business, project plans, detailed CVs for key players, your proposed schedule of payments, legal approval forms.

This is a large, rather indigestible meal, involving many hours of work, although some elements will be standard.

START WRITING AFTER THE FIRST MEETING

The rule about successful proposals is 'No surprises'.

The client needs to recognize 90 per cent of what you write and to have accepted it before the final draft. As the proposal elements are mutually exclusive, you can start working on all of them at the start, although you will reveal your thinking gradually. This means that, even after an initial meeting, you can summarize your understanding thus far. What is it about the client context that concerns them and is potentially driving their need for the solution?

Barbara Minto, author of *The Pyramid Principle*, a standard text for report writers, suggests a three-part approach to writing introductions for consulting reports: Situation, Complication, Question. The idea works for teeing up client needs, too:

1. The situation – this is what the steady state of your business, process or performance looked like.
2. Something happened to complicate this and cause a change: new regulations, more competition, technical advance – with the consequence that you now have...
3. A question about this issue: is it a problem or an opportunity? What is driving this issue? What could we do about it? Which option is best?

Defining client needs as questions is a good way to make them feel OK about the problem. Encourage them to clarify the exact questions when you next meet. Now you have something around which to frame your proposal that speaks to *them*, rather than being about your solution.

When the background issues, questions and client ambitions are clear, you can start to add information about their situation, challenging their view, perhaps, or comparing it with their competitors or the best player in their market. You can introduce research which you have done to highlight potential causes of this situation and future impacts, if nothing changes. Although you need to be careful not to appear too critical at any point in this part of the proposal, benchmarking their performance or showing trends in data they have provided you with (or even the range of feelings among stakeholders you have met about what action is appropriate) are all legitimate ways to increase the heat under their feet and establish that, even if the platform isn't yet burning, they have inadequate fire extinguishers.

OFFER ALTERNATIVES IN EARLY DRAFTS

There are many ways to achieve the outcomes that the client sees as desirable.

The seller's first challenge is to make the client realize that action isn't optional but mandatory. This is sometimes called 'showing the client the coffin' – you highlight what competitors are doing and what happens to companies who don't take action, using information from your research.

The second challenge is to confirm your company's commitment to helping the client. Successful sellers know that, even if they are ready to act, clients may not be ready to listen to a description of *the* correct solution (i.e. yours). One of the differences about selling solutions compared to products is that – except in situations you believe are real crises – you should not force closure on a client who is not yet ready to make the decision. Instead, offering alternatives leaves the client feeling in control of their destiny a while longer and demonstrates that your company's task is to act in a helpful way.

Choices encourage decisions. When people consider alternatives, the idea that they need not decide recedes. This is the opportunity to spell out the impact of each alternative in terms of the values of the outcomes they deliver and the potential risks involved. One approach is to present the options as a menu of solution elements, with escalating benefits and reducing risks. Another is to set up options at different levels of quality and cost ('platinum, gold and silver'). A third way is just to suggest how the same solution can be delivered differently: different timescales, different consortium partners, different management of the process.

The choice of options needs to honestly reflect the issues that you believe lie behind a broad acceptance of your solution and your company becoming the preferred partner of the client making the change. If, for example, you think that they are concerned that your company is too inexperienced, your options might include partnering with another supplier you know they trust. If they are concerned about cost, your options might be at different price points. If they are concerned about how long the implementation will take, you might include an option with increased rewards for hitting specific milestones.

LEAVE THE DETAILS UNTIL YOU KNOW THEIR BUDGET

Element 7 – the cost – is always at the back of your mind when selling. You have a target to hit, after all. 'How much are they good for?' in terms of investment in the project or solution is most logically discussed when they are considering options. Successful salespeople say that solutions selling, unlike product selling, isn't ultimately price sensitive, because, even if the elements are known, it is based on a value–delivery promise that is untested. If you can make the case for the value of the outcome and reassure them that you can deliver this reliably, then it becomes a discussion about return on investment, not price per se. Your clients will know what the market rate is for this sort of service and will be interested to know what the proposed alternatives might cost if they buy them from you. If you are near the market average, they may not negotiate. If they like your offer but see you as more expensive, they will.

So ask about their budget – either before working on the outline options or after you have presented them. Their budget-in-mind may not be what they tell you, of course, but an indication of price from the client is helpful in knowing whether this is mission impossible (withdraw and invest no more), mission possible (not quite what you were hoping, but not a total disaster) or mission really exciting (huge budget, relatively simple solution). This is not really a discussion about price, but a way of ensuring that before you do the detailed work on the rest of the proposal they are serious about spending some money.

Putting it all together

When considering seeking help with making a change, clients want to know about the solution, the provider and project contractual elements like cost and timetable. They often don't realize that the process of buying causes them to change their mind. When clients solicit multiple bids and talk with different providers, their ideas change about what outcomes they really want.

For this reason, proposal writing is a gradual process of educating the client, challenging their thinking and moving – with them – towards defining a solution or service that will deliver what they need.

29 NAMING THE PRICE IS NAMING THE VALUE

'Luxury goods prices are not directly linked to any type of costs. The art of luxury pricing lies in quantifying the value to consumer, regardless of cost, competitor or market prices.'
SKP marketing report

Price is the easy way to communicate what you know your service to be worth. Your price position ('premium expertise', 'best deal in town') says something about your brand, as well as the value you deliver. The lower end of the pricing spectrum targets millions of small business customers; the higher end is differently competitive – everybody is after the big guys' dollar.

Premium B2B solutions brands spend less on advertising and more on relationship building through helping their clients. Advertising creates recognition of your company's name and position; selling needs word of mouth. Referral clients come to you knowing approximately what you charge and you have an easier time telling them the number, assuming that the person who has referred you to them has shared this information. New clients that you have targeted and who have only accessed your website may have little idea what they may be in for. If they themselves are a premium brand – particularly if their line of business is anything like yours, services, solutions and the like – then this will also match their expectations.

A salesperson who sells a lot of consulting work into other professional services firms puts it like this:

'Our daily rates have to at least match theirs, depending on the level at which we are working. If we are running an offsite with 15 partners in the room, the opportunity cost to their business – assuming we can keep them in the room for a whole day – will be more than $75,000. If it's 15 managers, it's about $35,000. Add in a fancy venue and it soon adds up. If we ask for one-third of this opportunity cost, that's reasonable. If they blink, I just say, "You are investing $100k and I'm asking for one-quarter."'

Price naming is therefore about confidence in your own value as well as the real value to the client. When I train salespeople, I often ask them to name their actual cost to the client in terms of a daily rate. If you are doing the job right in the solutions world, your time does create value for your client as well as your company. Salespeople who have internalized a negative view of themselves find this particularly testing, just as junior professionals, when seeing their daily rate for the first time, feel it is hard to deliver this much value. In point of fact, most hourly and daily rates represent three times the actual value delivered; one-third for salary, one-third for overhead and one-third for profit.

GO FIRST WHEN NAMING THE PRICE – IT ANCHORS THE CLIENT'S THINKING

If you quote a number first, you get the advantage of 'anchoring' the client's thinking about price. But if the costs are going to be high, you probably don't want to alert them to how much they might have to pay and put them off. Often, the best way to answer the question 'What will it cost?' or 'How much do you charge?' is to provide examples of, say, a project you did for UNICEF and a service you provided for Citibank. This range demonstrates that what you are offering is not a product with a fixed price on a list but something that is adapted to the client's situation. Be prepared to account for the difference not just in terms of commercial benefit but also organizational and personal value created in the context. The message that you do 'pro bono' work at cost may also anchor client expectations about what they will have to pay, even as it demonstrates your company's social responsibility.

If the customer pushes you to be more specific about a particular solution or situation, you can mention time taken, number of people involved or other aspects of scale. Usually, at this stage your client will not know the exact scope of the work they need and neither may you. So you can offer a guide price range, based on assumptions which neither of you know to be true. I once won a large piece of work when after five minutes the target client asked me the price question outright. I replied, 'How much time do we need to make this happen?' He was canny enough to pass the question back to me and I honestly replied, 'Not less than three years from what you have told me about your business so far.' Later, he told me that all the other competing companies had said '18 months or less', which he knew from experience was impossible.

Here's a risky – but amusing – strategy, told me by a salesman who also worked as a stand-up. When asked 'How much...?' he would get out his calculator, input some figures, frown and say 'Hmmm... How does a million dollars sound to you?' Depending on the reaction (total incredulity, outrage, worried silence), he would either say 'Just joking...!' or... nothing. He never claimed to have sold his mid-range service for the cool million, but he did say it made clients open up in terms of their expectations. You can lose a project by being too cheap, of course; if the CEO has opined that this sort of transformation will 'need at least a $2 million investment' and your price is in the $500k range, you will not be seen as credible or 'understanding our need'.

Interestingly, when quoting the hypothetical million, my sales friend used a round number, which is never a good idea. A research project showed that when a battery was claimed to last 'up to two hours' customers predicted that it would last, on average, 89 minutes; when the same claim was presented as 'up to 125 minutes', customers' predictions rose to 106 minutes. Fine-grained units and numbers seem to help people to believe. Round numbers also suggest you may have rounded up, which can be taken as an invitation to negotiate. When people negotiate on round numbers they tend to use other round numbers, so bite off larger chunks. If your offer price is 375,000, presenting using integers such as 378,500 may provoke less negotiation and, if clients do, they may negotiate in smaller amounts. However, don't go for the 299.95 idea either, because this will place you in discount hell.

IF THEY DON'T DRAW BREATH, YOU PRICED TOO LOW

This is the so-called 'wince factor'. If, when you say the number the first time, the client doesn't look a bit taken aback, you are probably pitching it too low. If they don't wince, you can counter this with a suggestion such as 'This contract is very important to us; we want your business so we have priced accordingly.' (This might encourage the client to negotiate for a longer-term deal as they may consider you are hoping to win market share with a lower price. They expect you to try to raise prices over the terms of the contract.)

If they gasp and call for oxygen, then you need to counter this reaction with some comment suggesting negotiations ahead: 'Sadly, these days we have to price things so that your procurement function can get their pound of flesh.' If Procurement will not be involved, you then have a reason to reduce the price a bit.

And if the clients wince, well... you say nothing and just look enthusiastic about doing the work. 'Wow... well, that's a bit more than we were expecting...' (Silence.) 'To be honest, that's quite a bit more than we were expecting...' (Silence. Wait for them to ask.) 'Is this really what you charge?' ('Yes.') 'Is this your best price?' (Calmly, looking them straight in the eye: 'It is the price, yes.') And if they look as if this is a deal breaker, throw them a lifeline: 'This is not a very big job in our terms. Two years, scope more limited than we would recommend, a lot of real accountability and not much wiggle room. I guess you could say we have risk-based this price.'

Now we are into negotiation, but based on a good number to start with...

BE CONFIDENT ABOUT YOUR VALUE

This is the hard bit. Most professionals remember the day when they first discovered their hourly or daily rate and felt a bizarre mix of emotions: imposter insecurity, disbelief in the gullibility of their client, outrage at the exploitation of their talent (they weren't getting more than 20 per cent of this sum…). But both professionals and their solutions are increasingly valued in a world of self-service:

- First, you and your solution are focused on your client both by design and in service terms. Tailoring is expensive and you pay for the fit.
- Second, convenience is not cheap. Solutions make things easier for the client. They do part of the job for them. They take away either the sweat or the anxiety, or both.
- Thirdly, there are always unexpected benefits to every solution. Changing the organization is painful but it is a learning process for the client (as well as the provider). This learning has a value, too, which is why savvy clients negotiate on intellectual property rights at the start.
- Fourthly, you are good at what you do. Solutions are a competitive market and in a world where profits are increasingly hard to come by, expertise matched with a pleasant relationship is worth a lot more than you think. 'Pay peanuts, hire monkeys' is still true.

Putting it all together

If you don't quote a figure before they do, you lose the opportunity to anchor the discussion of price at some future point. For this reason, always pitch work with new clients high, as you can negotiate a lower unit cost in return for volume or a lower specification but you will find it hard to put the price up. Over time, clients expect discounts anyway.

Hold steady with their reaction. The 'pleasing' tendency of salespeople will not serve you well if you immediately offer them a price cut. If you know the value that your solution produces, why offer to increase that without something in return?

30 IN THE END, NICE GUYS CAN WIN

'You can't frighten people into taking a decision. If you raise their level of fear they can freeze, fight or flee. Persuasion requires positive emotion; measured optimism and interest in them, their situation and their challenges.'

Ian Bradley

Most organizations select suppliers using two methods. First, they agree some generic criteria for shortlisting proposals. The larger the group of people materially involved in the decision, the more generic and the less precise these criteria become. 'Offers excellent value for money' means nothing objectively but remains a popular criterion with larger groups. 'Meets technical specifications', 'Good fit with our culture'... terms like these are often so subjective that the shortlisting group have to give each proposal scores and then discuss what they meant by the number they assigned.

Like identifying the potential of a member of staff, past performance is not always a very reliable guide, but it is frequently the only guide the organization has when choosing a supplier. References, visits to other clients and pilot projects all relate to past performance. Services and solutions sales are future promises. Picking a company to provide a solution that, say, outsources a core function creates large amounts of risk for the client organization and for the decision-makers. What was an agreement in principle is now becoming an agreement in fact. Unsurprisingly, some groups founder altogether and don't appoint. They have too few objective yardsticks with which to compare the bids other than time and cost; the rest is reputation and past performance.

The final stage is to subject the shortlisted bidders to the 'beauty parade' – a chance to cross-examine the potential suppliers and find out what they are really made of. Whatever new intelligence this produces, the process helps the decision-making group hold each other accountable. 'Trial by jury' is generally seen as more reliable than the judgement of the individual. It also shares the blame. Unfortunately for the sales team, the jury is not a randomly selected bunch. They know one another and may have any number of relationship and power issues.

For a start, they have different interests in the purchasing decision. There have been various attempts to classify these roles, but it is clear that the people paying for the solution may not be those who stand to be affected most by its implementation on a day-to-day basis (even if they are overall accountable). Some people around the table will be looking at the bids from a specific perspective: technical competence, value-add to the business, impact on operations and so on. These perspectives inform what they see as the most important reason for choosing the winner. Sometimes a good chairperson will remind people of the fact that they will all be looking for something a bit different as a deciding factor.

All in all, the behaviour at 'beauty parades' can be as strange as the decisions they produce.

RELIABILITY MATTERS MORE THAN RELATIONSHIP TO THE PAYMASTER

The person sponsoring the change usually has the budget and their main concern is the reliability of the solution and the people delivering it. They will be comparing bidders based on the specification of the outcomes promised. They may also be interested in any risk-management elements in the contract, such as repayments for late delivery. They are bothered about the people involved only insofar as the solution relies on people to install, maintain and fix it.

If it does go wrong, they need to be sure that the whole group did a robust due diligence on the solution's reliability before they said yes, so this is the main focus of their questioning and debate. 'How do we know the solution will deliver?' They would rather not have a decision than go with the least-worst provider; they want to see confidence and a sensible commercial approach to managing any risks.

WORKING RELATIONSHIP MATTERS MOST TO THE STAKEHOLDERS

People directly affected by a major change are less idealistic. Everything will not work 100 per cent on day one. Things never do. They have been through many such changes before and... very few work well at the start.

These stakeholders' prime concern is therefore the vendor's people who will be working on the solution – their attitude, their professionalism, their decency. If they are alienating, irritating, impatient or arrogant, stakeholders like this will prefer another bidder. They aren't competent to decide which solution is technically better – that will be for others. But they can distinguish arrogance from confidence.

INTELLIGENCE OR TECHNICAL BRILLIANCE IS OFTEN SECONDARY TO BOTH

The excellence of the solution is not without importance in the beauty parade decision. The leading technical adviser on the options presented – sometimes an external consultant – will be invited to offer an opinion, and this opinion may be used to exclude one or more of the bidders, but not to choose between the final two (unless the group cannot reach agreement). Second-best technologies often win popular approval based on user criteria – like simplicity of functionality – and this idea sometimes appears in the jury discussions, because technology is generally seen as the servant of the business and not the other way around. 'As long as it will work...', somebody says and the rest nod. This is often where the final conversation about technical differences (which are actually objective points of comparison) tends to start and end.

What does all this mean for how you should handle beauty parades? A salesperson explains their approach:

'When you go to the beauty parade they are looking at you as much as the solution. They usually reckon they have done the due diligence on this beforehand. So you don't have a majority of technical specialists making the decision. That's why it's called the beauty parade. You need to present the team. You won't have a very long time as the audience has usually made up their mind as individuals; they just need a shared experience from which to make up their minds as a group. It's going to be down to subjective factors, if your price is not way off. They will have told you if you are much more expensive beforehand, so you will have been given the chance to adjust it. The things that go wrong are legion; our technical guy gets into an argument with their technical guy; their project manager insists that a timescale won't work. These are all things that can easily be fixed, but people forget. How we respond to these challenges are indications to the client about what it will be like for them if they give us the project. I tell everybody, "Be positive, and take a 'can do' attitude to any issue." *Any* issue. It's the best policy.'

Putting it all together

Just because your offer is the most intelligent doesn't mean it will win. The subjective process of comparing bidders means that you will be subject to the winds of politics, because any solution bid represents change.

The best bet seems to be to understand the different constituencies represented in the room and make sure that you address their concerns. But the main message from experienced and successful salespeople is that in this lottery nice guys might actually come first.

Final tip: go first if you are the incumbent or market leader. Go last if you are the upstart. The 'recency' effect seems to influence decisions.

DISCIPLINE WORKS BETTER THAN LUCK

'Day by day, what you do is who you become.'
Heraclitus

Successful salespeople are disciplined in the way they do their job. When you see a salesperson who appears to be extraordinarily lucky, it is usually the result of hard work and operating to a set of clear principles – like any other kind of success. One survey of salespeople showed that:

- 48 per cent of salespeople never follow up a lead
- 25 per cent of salespeople make a second contact and stop
- 12 per cent of salespeople make only three contacts.

Only 2 per cent of sales are closed on first contact, 3 per cent on second contact, 5 per cent on third contact, 10 per cent on fourth contact and 80 per cent of sales are made on the fifth to the twelfth contact.

These sorts of facts suggest that discipline matters.

The person who suggested this secret was extraordinarily well organized. An advocate of sales force software, his diary and address book were immaculate. He set himself targets for emails and phone calls every day and meetings every week. Knowing his conversion rates, he could fairly reliably predict the number of proposals he would write every month and often the number of wins. He had an assistant with whom he worked closely over many years in terms of setting up appointments and checking on people's availability. He very rarely wasted time with calls that got cancelled. He never forgot important details because he used his diary to remind himself of any commitment he – or his clients – made. And if he ever had a spare minute he would do something personal for a client.

It is interesting to compare his system with the world's greatest car salesman, a guy called Joe Girard who sold on average five cars per day. According to the *Guinness Book of Records*, he sent out 146,000 postcards to customers every year. The cards just read, 'I like you.' That took some organizing.

DECIDE ON YOUR PRIORITIES AND STICK TO THEM

If you have a target, divide this number by the average order size in your business. Then consider what your conversion rate is – the ratio of lead meetings to sales closed, not proposals to sales closed – and work out how many meetings that means in the time period. Then you know how many meetings you should aim for per month and this will probably relate to the number of contacts you make. This is the basic activity planning which underpins all successful selling over time. This is what people mean when they say selling is 'a numbers game'.

Prioritize your targets. The basis for this depends on your solutions and your markets, but establish some principles based on the experience of the sales team. For example:

- **First tier** – big needs, big budgets (growing fast, market leaders, lots of competition and takes a long time to close). Best for leading-edge solutions which give the client competitive advantage to stay ahead, and also for products that are sold only to one company in each sector (e.g. loyalty reward systems)
- **Second tier** – doing well; not that fashionable but a steady performer. Best for other long-standing businesses as suppliers with a wide range of operational improvement solutions. Not a strategic sell, but regular renewals
- **Third tier** – family mid-size businesses...

and so on.

Have clear priorities for leads as they proceed through the funnel. This makes sure that your cost of sales reflects the potential value of the contract. Essentially, you need to decide at each stage in the funnel (lead, prospect, qualified prospect) which aspects of the contract will cause you to:

- prioritize the sale and invest more rapidly
- allow the client to make the running
- drop the project.

How much you invest will depend on the margins on your solutions, but if your margin was, say, 30 per cent, you might invest 15 per cent of the total contract size on winning a new, strategically important client. If your margins are much smaller, you would still invest up to 50 per cent of that margin in a new client. Tracking cost of sales is important to ensure that you are not wasting time or money; the salesperson's time is rarely accounted for but is a significant cost to your business. Comparing your hourly cost to a senior specialist can produce some interesting results!

Usually, salespeople want to win big and early and the potential size of the deal is the first criteria for continuing to invest in the sale. Criteria that are based on the value of the contract to your business will depend on what sort of business *you* are in. Common criteria across all solutions providers include:

- contract value (revenues, longer-term value)
- client value (loyal client, new client, board-level client, strategically important client)
- the nature of the contract itself (key bridgehead sale in new sector, chance to develop new intellectual property, 'turnkey' solution).

Criteria about the sort of solution the client is interested in may also reflect what your aims are as a business; for example, a strategy consulting firm wanting more long-term revenues might prioritize projects which also have tricky organizational implementation issues, as this enables them to sell on other work.

KEEP YOUR PRODUCT AND SECTOR KNOWLEDGE FRESH

Selling with a system helps to get you organized, but solutions selling requires you to consciously refresh your knowledge of markets and competitors' products. Some of this will be learned on the road, listening to clients, or from colleagues, but it is easy to get behind the curve on the latest thinking. Clients for solutions are getting more sophisticated, everybody says. There are increasingly fewer places for the smoke and mirrors in solution selling.

But new thinking and ideas are always being created. Since salespeople travel a lot, there is usually time to catch up by reading journals and books about your client's sector, and more broadly about business. Competitive advantage and market share are crucial for businesses in times of slower growth, so understanding what these mean – and how they relate to your solution – is important.

Clients also expect you to understand the wider market that they are looking at to purchase a solution they have in mind. They may ask your opinion and, although you can sometimes get away with 'We don't comment on our competitors', a knowledge of the features and prices of your rival's offerings is important to being able to promote what you offer in their place. Clients will be particularly well read on industry reports that compare solutions and products. The Internet has meant that clients can be as well informed about the options as you. This can be disconcerting and they will like to test business, market and product knowledge with such innocent questions as 'What did you think about that article about CAD systems in last month's *Economist*?'

DON'T BECOME A BORE

Disciplined mustn't mean boring and incapable of acting spontaneously, because every minute is accounted for. Most people dedicate 80 per cent of their time to work and 20 per cent of their time to family life, leaving precisely no time for themselves, and then wonder why they have nothing to talk about except work. The great thing about selling is that, when the target is in sight, so are holidays and time to refresh your thinking in other ways, such as going to exhibitions or fixing up that bike.

Successful salespeople are personally more interested in a wide range of things and often have rather enviable lifestyles based on being able to walk away from the company when the task is done. This makes them interesting to others and good to spend time with. If you feel you are getting boring, you probably are, and you will not be able to entertain your clients with amusing anecdotes from your life outside work.

Putting it all together

Disciplined and dedicated are the means but not the end of great selling.

Salespeople love to 'wing it', often to get the buzz of adrenalin excitement which, for many salespeople, is their avowed motivation. While this is all right (sometimes) in face-to-face situations, it is no way to ensure that you meet your target. For that you need a system and there are plenty of sales manuals around which preach a specific system for success.

Keep your self-organization in balance with time to develop interesting ways of building conversations and relationships.

32 TWO EARS, TWO EYES AND ONE MOUTH

'I was so sure that I knew what they needed and what I wanted to sell them that I never stopped to find out what they wanted to buy.'
Chris Murray

The behaviour most associated with trust is listening. It demonstrates:

- interest
- care and concern
- readiness to subordinate your own feelings and needs to those of the other person.

I have heard this idea recommended so regularly that it seems as if the salespeople were having to remind themselves of its importance. It is also extremely hard for well-trained salespeople to do. Classic sales training focuses on scripts and pitches and handling objections. I once asked my dentist how much time in her lengthy qualification process had been spent on understanding the psychology of pain. 'About 45 minutes,' she said. The proportion of time spent on listening and giving people feedback on the quality of their listening in sales school is not that dissimilar.

Great salespeople, like great negotiators, know the power of silence. The desire to speak is about our nervousness and our desire to look good, not about helping the client to clarify what outcomes they really need. Remember the coffee cup test of a good sales call: when their cup is full and cold and yours is empty.

Putting it all together

Ears, eyes, mouth – in that order.

33 CAVEAT VENDITOR

'Always have a vision; be passionate, act confident even when you're not; think of it as you want it to be, not as it is; don't let others sway you from your point of view; see things in the present even if they are in the future; don't give others your power.'
Philip Delves Broughton

According to the researcher Galen Bodenhausen, people in a room with a mirror are less likely to cheat or show racial or gender prejudice, and they are more likely to be helpful and work hard: 'When people are made to be self-aware, they are likelier to stop and think about what they are doing.'

But the rules of buying and selling are often thought to operate to a different moral compass. If the common aim is to win, one party has to lose, and both parties will be circumspect about providing the other with information that might put them at a disadvantage. Everybody knows about the Prisoner's Dilemma experiment, which demonstrates that collaboration produces a better result, but this doesn't necessarily mean that buyers and sellers act in accordance with that finding. Actually, *neither* side likes to share the full picture of their environment, or how it will affect their decisions and other behaviour.

Clients we know hold back on:

- the size of their budget
- their measures for comparing the bids
- (sometimes) the decision-making process
- Procurement's targets.

Salespeople we know hold back on:

- their company's business model
- the true costs of design and delivery
- (sometimes) the risks for clients

- other clients' business issues
- their sales targets in terms of revenues and margin.

When there is a framework agreement in place – as with certain suppliers in, say, the automotive and defence industries – many of these areas become more transparent. Japanese car manufacturers help their suppliers to build factories in the same location and government procurement has to have long-term contracts of trust to deal with the degree of uncertainty that accompanies the creation of a complex product like a new fighter jet. 'Open book accounting' – the mutual sharing of cost information – does happen, for example when intermediaries are tasked with doing some of the procurement deals for the company. The agreement is then around acceptable levels of margin at different points in the contract, not the overall price. You cannot run this without shared data, which is becoming increasingly easy to access.

The net of all this can be that people become cynical about others' motives. Cynicism corrodes relationship cogs, as optimism oils its wheels. Of course, both parties should be sceptical, because this may lead to a better result all round. They should ask testing questions. They should state their requirements based on their past experience. Lack of discussion and transparency about important matters often affects the delivery of the solution. The salesperson and the buyer need to address this as part of the sale. *Caveat emptor* is also *caveat venditor*.

BE OPEN ABOUT WHAT INFORMATION YOU WILL SHARE WITH YOUR PROSPECT

If you are responding to an RFP, there may already be some 'rules' about disclosure of information at different stages in the buying process, with written safeguards built in to protect the client's business interests. In the same way, your company should be clear about what you are prepared to give the client access to, and when. Terms and conditions of business relate to selling as well as delivery; what level of transparency gives your company an advantage? Most sellers aim to be as transparent about their business as possible to build confidence, but it is important to decide where the no-go areas might be – information about other clients particularly.

If you have initiated the sale, this is doubly important, as both parties will be testing each other out more vigorously. Once the client agrees that there may be a need you can help them with, they are accepting that the relationship is moving to a different level of trust. You don't want them at this point to come up with the bright idea of an RFP, so the more you work with the sponsors and stakeholders the longer this may be delayed (until or unless the bid is so large that Procurement must be involved). Suggesting you sign a non-disclosure agreement might give you some advantage.

PROTECT INTELLECTUAL PROPERTY UNLESS YOUR BUSINESS IS INTELLECTUAL

Nobody gives away the code that lies behind their software, obviously. But there are situations where your intellectual property needs to be experienced before the client will consider hiring you.

Advisory work is often called 'vapourware' by the technicians because it doesn't do anything. Except that it does: it changes minds and helps people feel more confident about making decisions. If your business is an advisory service rather than a solution that is mostly product, then intellectual property is what you sell. Your client will want evidence of what you have done before: analytical reports and so on. You will need to have redacted versions of these to demonstrate your quality as part of the sales process.

Ultimately, your client may well request that, if they hire you, they share joint ownership of, say, the analytical models which your firm provides. This is like asking for the software of the system and you need to be careful about the terms under which you agree to such things. Generally, the rule is that if they use it for their own purposes it is different from if they use it for financial gain, although this is difficult to establish with intellectual property such as training materials, where the *point* of the service is to educate widely.

HANDLE REQUESTS FOR COMMERCIAL DATA CAREFULLY

Anxious clients may be interested in your company's performance, to ensure that you will be reliable. You may be expected to provide your turnover for the last few years or numbers of professionals employed, which is easy if you are a public company but less so if you are a privately owned partnership. Some sectors also like the reassurance that you know their business, so would like to know clients in the sector for whom you have worked. However, a list of clients doesn't mean a lot unless you have worked with them for several years and they have agreed to act as references, so be careful whom you nominate.

Depending on the solution you offer, you may be expected to provide reference sites and performance information, which the customer can check with an existing client. This is often difficult because the performance of any solution is rarely wholly under your control; there may be mitigating circumstances relating to the wider economy or – more tricky to explain – the behaviour of the client organization. In such cases, the initial assumptions about the conditions behind the predicted performance (at the time of buying) need to be compared with the actual conditions you have found. The key is to do this as simply as possible so that the client doesn't feel you are being tricky. That often means taking legal advice before you start.

And what if you have no relevant data about the solution? What if it is brand new and this is the first client you have approached? General data about your business is still relevant – turnover, staff, customers – but specific data about the performance of the solution will not be available. You may have data from pilot projects and you need to get a reference site going as soon as possible, so some element of risk/reward payment may be necessary first time around. Here again, relationships will be critical; if you have a customer who is very satisfied with what you have delivered in the past, they may be more open to a 'pilot' programme. A brand-new client with a brand-new solution is as unlikely as a swarm of bees in winter.

Putting it all together

Being wary makes good business sense, because even if your values and intentions as a business are clear, those of your client may not be. You have only to have one bad debt to learn that terms and conditions of business have to be signed by both parties. While you obviously need to remain cautious about legal and contractual matters, employing a specialist if necessary, this should not inform the whole way in which you communicate and relate to the client.

The rule, if it can be called this, is to be as transparent as you can about everything. Exaggeration, false claims and false testimonials end up causing problems to all concerned and harm your reputation in the market. Agreeing the process of gradually sharing information with your client makes sense to both parties and avoids cynicism on both sides.

HOW YOU FEEL IS PART OF HOW YOU WIN

'I've learned that people will forget what you said, people will forget what you did, but people will never forget how you made them feel.'
Maya Angelou

Selling is emotionally hard, with highs and lows in rapid succession. When your offer is rejected, it is difficult not to take this personally; you invested time and effort and emotion in constructing a good deal. Clients can be rude and offensive in the way they behave and the salesperson is 'fair game' in many organizations. Many salespeople deal with the rejections and emotional challenges of the job by telling themselves it's just a game or a role they play.

Coaching people in sales has shown me that strategies to protect yourself and your emotions have some gender bias, with men preferring to think of themselves as participants in a game and women more engaged with the idea that this is a part they play. While I have no statistical evidence for this, the way people cope with rejection seems to differ. One saleswoman said:

'I'm not really like this. At the weekend, with my daughters and the horses, you wouldn't even notice me. At work I put on the clothes and the make-up and step out on to the stage and do my thing. I know how to attract attention and I use it. But actually I'm quite a shy person.'

And a salesman expressed it by saying:

'I don't get too stressed about losing, even if I'm selling to people I think of as friends. We are both playing to win and that element of competition makes the game enjoyable. You have to separate relationships from the game when you're selling. It's just business.'

Successful salespeople see themselves not so much as a performer but more of an athlete, somebody who adapts their equipment and approach to the competition, the weather and the track. They behave in ways that they think will work with *this* customer. They couch what they say with this aim in mind, so they are trying to manage the situation. But they also manage to retain a large amount of personality in the relationship. They are prepared to put who they are at risk, for the sake of a sale. That takes courage and professionalism.

The skilful use of self in selling is complex. It is about your identity and how strong you feel emotionally. But real, long-term relationships are not always emotional walks in the park. So this will be a choice.

MAKE SURE THAT YOUR INITIAL 'CHAT' IS EMOTIONALLY OPEN AND ENGAGING

What do you say as you shake the customer's hand? Make it an authentic reflection of what has led up to this meeting.

If you finally get to meet the target after several cancellations by the client, you might say:

'Thanks for making the time to see me. You must get a lot of people trying to get into your diary, so I really appreciate this.'

If a colleague or mutual acquaintance has referred you to this person, you might say:

'Thanks for seeing me. John thought we should meet and I'm very glad you agreed... [The client seems impatient.] ... You're busy, I can see, so let's cut to the chase. What – if anything – did John tell you about me or the company?'

If you are revisiting a client you haven't seen for a while, you might say:

'How are you? How's business? I'm sorry not to have been in touch for – what is it? – nearly a year. We have been [e.g. super busy]. How's business here?'

Written down like this, everything looks like a script but that isn't the point. The remarks need to be a spontaneous reaction, expressive of positive emotion. All that talk about golf handicaps and traffic on the motorway is noise. The point of the meeting is to find – or develop – an idea for improving your client's business, and, in the process, yours. Personal stuff is for later, when each of you has done the initial qualification of the other and you want to oil the wheels of the working relationship. So getting too personal too soon is inappropriate.

Ask yourself, 'How am I feeling? How is the client likely to be feeling? What element of how I am feeling should I disclose, to come across as authentic and professional?'

WHEN YOU PARAPHRASE OR SUMMARIZE, BE HONEST

After the discussion about the client's context and issues, think about summarizing what you have heard. As you do so, add some insight but also some emotional reaction. I sat in on the first meeting between an adviser and a new client. The client has just given an overview of the background to the business situation; the consultant had also been involved in a start-up. The consultant then says:

'That's a great story. May I just summarize what you have told me to ensure I've got this right? After ten years both the retail and the club businesses have grown in line with what you had hoped, but you are still more "hands on" than you would perhaps ideally like to be – partly because of the difficulty you have in finding people to do the things you have done so successfully over the years – selling, marketing and brand management. I can sympathize with that; we had very similar issues in our company. I read a report by KPMG which highlighted the growing issue of creating a talent pipeline in most developed economies, but didn't really identify any underlying causes, other than a severe lack of joined-up HR data analytics with which to manage this issue. It's a bit of a ticking time bomb, particularly in this country. So why? Why is it hard to solve the succession problem in your company?'

The client gives his reasons: no time to think about these medium- to longer-term issues, no professional HR person in the company of 100, perhaps a certain preference to personally retain control over a function in the company. The consultant responds by saying:

'It's hard to let go. And it can be the case in second-stage businesses that founders, completely unintentionally, hold back the development of their companies. Like parents [he's spotted the photos so he knows the client has children] during their children's adolescence. Sort of too protective but also worried about the empty nest. What are your plans to deal with this issue here?'

Personal and professional are not incompatible if you are that sort of person, which most good salespeople are.

TALK ABOUT YOUR EMOTIONAL REACTIONS AS YOU WOULD TO A FRIEND

At the end of the meeting, the conversation usually diverts into next steps, plans and pleasantries. You have just taken up an hour of the client's time. At more senior levels this could have cost the company many hundreds of dollars. Depending on how the meeting has gone, you might reflect on it in different, emotionally authentic ways.

If it has been a great meeting, with good chemistry and also interesting conversation with at least a couple of topics you can follow up on, you might now say something like:

'James. Very good to meet you and thanks again. This has been really great. I'm going to go away and think about what we have discussed and, if it's OK with you, will send you those statistics we talked about. I'd also like to follow this up by talking with some other people here, if you are amenable to that idea. It's an area I'm very interested in. Without obligation, of course: at this point neither of us knows where this might lead. It's ambiguous, which I still find rather exciting. Could I ask my assistant to contact yours to set this up? I'll email you a rough outline of an agenda and maybe you can suggest two or three people I could meet. And then you and I can meet again to discuss the results and see what's what.'

If it has been rather an awkward meeting, with not much chemistry, but the client definitely needs what your company could help with, you might say:

'OK. This has been most helpful to me – and I hope a bit to you? I've learned a lot, so thanks. Is there anything we have discussed that you would like to follow up on? [Rhetorical] You seemed interested in the discussion about the software... and also the project management processes that underpin the design. From what you said, you are already taking both these things very seriously, but maybe a meeting with one of my technical colleagues could help build on your company thinking? I'd be very happy to arrange that, if you feel that it would be of interest. Maybe with your IT manager?'

If the meeting has had good chemistry but there is nothing your company can really assist with now, you might say:

'Thank you, James. Lovely to meet you. All that information you provided. A great achievement. You sound as if you are in good shape on most of the areas we discussed. Really. You are in good shape on most aspects of [data storage] compared to lots of people I call on. Which from my perspective is a little disappointing for now, but going forward... I'm sure we can find new ways to help you do things faster, better, cheaper... who knows? I'm wondering if you, or one of your staff, would like to make a trip to our lab? Find out about what we are working on next? I'd be glad to arrange this as a bit of a "thank you" for giving me your time.'

Putting it all together

Revealing yourself is tough, but emotion is the way we connect at a human level. It supersedes all barriers of role, seniority and culture. Even pre-language-age babies have been shown to react to 17 emotions in their parents; we are just hard-wired to be sentient.

Successful salespeople read the signs and are emotionally honest about the way they communicate with clients. It takes courage, because when we are authentic the inevitable rejections are harder to absorb. And it takes even greater courage to remain emotionally authentic as the years go by. This may be a good reason to find clients you enjoy working with and stick with them.

35 SPONTANEITY TAKES PRACTICE

'Sales are contingent upon the attitude of the salesman, not the attitude of the prospect.'
W. Clement Stone

Here's a story I was told by a successful salesman about his boss, Tim, when he was just the bag-carrying rookie. The experience clearly made a big impression on him, as it had taken place over 20 years before:

'We were pitching to Unilever in a meeting room on the 15th floor, floor-to-ceiling plate glass windows with a breathtaking view of the Thames. Everything was going wrong. They sat there. No reaction. But we battled through to the end. Silence. You could hear a pin drop. So my boss Tim said, "We may not be winning this business, but I would sure as hell love your window-cleaning contract." We had nothing to lose. They laughed. We could start again.'

The ability to seize the moment is heady stuff, the stuff of legends. You may wonder whether such an event really occurred. (I often wonder this when listening to salespeople describing their feats of daring.) But even if it is only a parable, it is worth telling. It says that spontaneity can help you to win.

People often imagine that spontaneity is a function of personality, a sort of chutzpah, a kind of courage, potentially a mild form of insanity, as it appears to take a massive risk with what has already been gained to just push the client a bit further. Actually, your ability to be in the moment can be learned and it improves with practice.

How can you practise being spontaneous? It sounds like a contradiction. Actors have to learn to improvise as well as speak from scripts. They learn it by adhering to a few simple skills, which underpin good (i.e. compelling, memorable) improvisation. These skills include:

- trust in the other actors to support you – the ability to make yourself vulnerable to your colleague's skill
- suspension of the civilized tendency to self-censor – the ability to do or say the first thing rather than the more considered option
- acceptance of other actors' ideas ('offers' as they are called) – the ability to build on others' ideas and behaviour using the 'Yes, and…' approach
- awareness of others – the ability to acutely observe and listen
- mastery of narrative – a continuous sense of 'where this might be going'
- presence and status in performance – the ability to attract attention.

Not all of these are equally applicable in sales situations, although many of these skills will help to bridge the customer/ supplier gap by giving you a sense of working 'with'. They can all be improved with practice and review.

PLAY WITH THE IDEA OF VULNERABILITY AND SEE WHAT HAPPENS

As already noted, the ability of clients to trust you is in part a function of perceived risks in the situation. Your ability to trust them is also about perceived risks. But if you focus on the emotion of vulnerability, you may notice that many of the risks are imagined rather than real. How are you feeling? Why are you feeling vulnerable (if you are)? What is the worst that can happen from this meeting? It is probably that the conversation goes nowhere, for now, or that they show you the door before the agreed time – or even, potentially, that you do not get any chemistry going with them at all.

What happens if you flip all this on its head? What happens if you trust your client's goodwill? One of the techniques used to direct actors to manage their behaviour is not to instruct them to 'act more confident', or to 'act more bravely' but rather that you give them a presupposition about the other character: 'She is frightened but doesn't show it' or 'He has no chance of winning this fight'. The actor's behaviour – increased confidence or bravery – becomes a response to a supposition and flows more naturally. If you apply this to your own situation with clients, you behave differently, more trustingly. Tell yourself that the client is not actually a critical or judgemental person but that they have reasons – problems and issues – that account for their behaviour, no matter how difficult. They want the best from this conversation, as you do. Negative behaviour is not about you; it is about them.

What tends to happen when you make this assumption is that you are more relaxed, less guarded, more open, feeling less 'on trial' and more fun to be with. This person is like a colleague who shares the same goals. You are working together on something. You can be spontaneous.

BUILD ON THE CLIENT'S OWN IDEAS AND DON'T INTERRUPT THEIR THINKING

In B2B service-selling situations, your solution is capable of many variations. The deal can be constructed in many different ways. When a client objects, they are giving you information about something they would value more than the offer you are currently making, not criticizing you or your offer. When you welcome this (spontaneous?) reaction from the client and build on it, you are heading off in a different direction, one which might be more valuable, not just for them but also for you. If their issue is genuine (not just a negotiation tactic), try saying something like:

- 'That's an interesting observation. And we understand that. And we would add that...'
- 'True. What's more...'
- 'Yes. I think I see that. Say more about that...'

This aspect of spontaneity goes against the 'control the sale' messages that you carry in your head, *but* if you think about where that comes from, it belongs in the world of scripts, not improvisation, which is where most successful salespeople now live. When you are in a play and your fellow actor forgets a line or suddenly does a speech from Act Two, you have to find a way to get the show back on track, but in improvisation this diversion is seen as positive, leading to an even broader seam of gold than the one you were just mining.

Of course, all this sounds risky, but if you want to be more 'in the moment' then you have to experiment.

BE CLEAR ABOUT THE NARRATIVE IN WHAT IS HAPPENING

In the scripted product world, controlling the sale meant controlling the discourse. If the customer says this, you say that. If they make this objection, we offer this rebuttal. 'These are the five main reasons to do business with us...' 'These are the three messages we need to communicate in our pitch.'

In the less structured, more relationship-based solutions world, we try to control the sale by narrative. In improvisational terms, this means working out where you are heading with this improvisation. Of course, different actors in the improvisation will have a different storyline in mind and part of the fun for the audience is watching the players twist the narrative and then have to respond to the other actors' offers.

In business, this would be frustrating if it carried on too long, but there are basic narrative 'arcs' in the start of most sales situations. Here are some examples:

- A stable situation becomes less stable, leaving the client with a challenge and a quest to find an answer. The salesperson is a person she trusts.

- A decision to make a change has been taken but the client does not know how to deliver this change and wants to find alternatives. He is asking several salespeople's advice.
- The client is new to the organization and sees opportunities that her colleagues do not realize. She needs to find a way to alter their scepticism about the possibilities and, coincidentally, a salesperson's contact arrives on the day she has to deal with this.
- The client has no idea about a missed opportunity and nor does his company. He is reluctant to put current performance at risk for the sake of a potentially better future because he is approaching retirement. Enter a salesperson with new thinking.

When in this situation of narrative ambiguity, improvisers often test out their own understanding by asking questions of the other actors. ('So we are off to the zoo now, are we?' 'What happened to your mother-in-law when you jumped off the cliff?' 'Am I supposed to fly the plane?') In sales situations we also need to check out what the customer's narrative-in-mind may be, while expressing ours. ('I get a sense of urgency about this. Do you feel this conversation is helping you clarify your thinking?' 'Where would you like to take this next?' 'I think the next step should be a joint meeting with your boss.')

Just as there are acts in plays, there are acts in sales situations:

- Act One: client in state of ignorance, alerted by some incident (bad quarter's results, new boss, salesperson's contact)
- Act Two: client sets out on journey to discover causes and effects, current situation and potential solutions (hopefully with you)
- Act Three: clash of the titans – client has to choose the best proposal (hopefully yours)

Practise thinking about this by reflecting on past (successful) sales narratives and using these to shape the narrative options with existing clients.

Putting it all together

The ability to be spontaneous takes practice because it takes confidence to go in a creative direction and to feel that you can create a sensible narrative with your client. They say that pre-prepared jokes are the death of real improvisation, but sometimes prepared elements – the equivalent of props – are useful. The salesperson who leaps up and says, 'Can I just draw something on your white board?' and then produces a neat piece of her company's intellectual property made relevant to the clients in the room is always more impressive than the same idea on a PowerPoint slide. 'Did she think about doing this before? Does she always do this in client meetings?' is what runs through clients' heads.

But actually it doesn't matter. The spontaneous offer of a new way of looking at the issues illuminates and the client, improvising in turn, will build on the gift. 'Yes... and...' Isn't that what you want to happen?

36 SALES TEAMS NEED CHOCOLATE

'No man is an island entire of itself.'
John Donne

Selling used to be a solo performance, and in many companies this aspect of the job is still reinforced with competition and awards for individuals who achieve results. The old model was a lonely road and it appealed to individuals who were happier in the hotel than at the office, who perhaps convinced themselves and their families that this was a better life they were providing than the office nine-to-five. The tools were samples and other marketing collateral – all branded – and the laptop was preloaded with spreadsheets and price lists. Your car or the airport lounge was your home. It was often a dull existence, enlivened by the occasional drama of a big pitch to a client, a test of the salesperson's quality and skills.

It worked because the decision-makers were generally other individuals and what you sold could be demonstrated, sampled or test-driven in some way.

Solutions aren't bought like this. As decisions tend to be made in groups, solutions buying has become a team activity. As solutions require a range of specialists to work together with people on the client side, the delivery team is part of the decision to buy. As solutions can change the way the client business operates over the medium term, clients need to experience the reliability and skills of the people who will do this.

The solo salesperson still has to open the can. But the meal is cooked and served by the team.

CHOOSE AND DEVELOP YOUR TEAM
OF ANALYSTS

Some organizations have a pool of researchers who are available
to all salespeople and will – to the limit of their resources – do
whatever preparation work the salesperson wants from them.
Often, this marketing collateral about the solution is developed
for all the people involved in going to market with the solution;
it is of necessity about the solution and possibly the industry
towards which the solution is aimed. It is rarely about the
specific client, unless the salesperson commissions the researcher
to do this.

Successful salespeople are good at creating loyalty – among
the research community in their company as much as with
clients. They spot the high-flyers in sales support and cultivate
the relationship with them. It helps if they themselves are
successful, because all researchers or sales analysts like to
be involved in successful campaigns. But, more than that, it
helps if the salesperson takes a real managerial interest in the
junior – providing ideas for research, allowing them to present
to the client where possible and giving them feedback. In
short, they are educating them so that they can be promoted.

Since selling is externally focused, salespeople can forget the
value to them of this loyalty. Are they themselves a good team
player? This was never a criterion for recruitment in the past,
which is why great salespeople are often bad sales managers.
They prefer the lonely road and the occasional glory. But in
solutions the bench strength of the whole sales function becomes
important for the success of the individual.

DEVELOP A STRONG NETWORK OF SPECIALISTS
IN DELIVERY

Clients are not that interested in meeting the analysts, although
they will want to know results, but they are very interested
in anybody who will be working with their people: project

managers, developers and specialists. Some of these experts will be more client-friendly than others and they will be in strong demand from everyone working in sales. As their primary responsibility is delivery, engaging them in your selling effort takes... well, selling.

What makes a good specialist to add to your sales 'team', virtual or actual? Most of those interviewed agree that responsiveness and an interest in business development are key criteria for spotting a good sales partner. Often, this will be someone who is interested in developing their own sales skills or in a career shift in your direction, too. Such people will always be in demand for client meetings. The least good candidates are those who have poor social skills – even though they may be brilliant – and who will not respond to coaching about how to handle the meeting. Clients are quite understanding of strangeness and brilliance but prefer it to be packaged in a staff-friendly way.

Why would these relatively scarce types want to work for you on a bid? Just because they have a performance objective that says they should is rarely motivation enough. Exposure to new clients is often the opportunity to do interesting technical work and specialists often enjoy these challenges. Standard implementations do not give you much chance to influence the work you are given, but working from the start on a bid just might. In other words, being part of the sales effort ultimately could give preferential access to the more interesting work which you have had a hand in scoping. However, the salesperson needs to be able to guarantee that 'involvement equals being first choice to deliver'. This is sadly not always the case – utilization management being what it is – but if you can secure this agreement you may find it easier to enrol the specialist you want.

GIVE CREDIT TO THE TEAM

Many junior analysts and senior specialists are not that happy to become involved in selling, for the following reasons:

- It interferes with the day job – their involvement may be prescribed but is stressful nonetheless.
- They don't much benefit; the salesperson gets the bonus, not them.

You need to be sure that, as far as you can, you are working to change both these factors, if this problem exists in your company. The first reason is often a reflection about how organized the salesperson is and how well they are controlling the client/the sale. This is not easy to do, as clients will do what clients will do during the sales process and they can be difficult to pin down to a timetable that makes it easier for others to participate.

'I usually sell a meeting with the best specialist (with their prior knowledge) and then say they are extremely busy working on another contract so are only available on a Friday, which is their day in the office. This raises the client's expectations about quality and limits their expectations about access. It also helps the specialists to be available if Friday is their day in the office. I also speak with their project managers to find out where the really critical points are in their current projects. That helps, too.'

Many service and solutions providers don't like the idea of sharing the rewards and recognition for selling, as a way of reinforcing the salesperson's responsibility for delivering. The partnership structure is particularly prone to this; the message given is that 'One day, if you make partner, you will be well rewarded, so for now, keep your head down.' This might have worked in a world of apprenticeships but isn't wildly appealing to anybody under 30, who will expect a more egalitarian approach. Jam tomorrow? I'd rather start my own business. So, as a minimum, all people involved in a successful bid should be credited by name and take part in any celebration at the kick-off of the project. If you can arrange some even nominal financial reward, so much the better. It is about fairness rather than a gross amount for most people.

Putting it all together

Whether your sales team is actual – for large bids – or not, many salespeople need the goodwill participation of the people whose skills and services they sell in order to achieve the sale. Unlike with clients, where charm may go a long way to get what you want, colleagues are not so easy to sell to. There has to be a win for them in this participation – at a minimum some utilization but also some credit and some benefit in terms of project work.

Salespeople cannot assume that specialists will just help. There has to be an exchange of goodwill.

**ENERGY IS
NEITHER
CREATED NOR
DESTROYED**

*'To achieve great things, two things are needed; a plan, and
not quite enough time.'*
Leonard Bernstein

Selling is tiring, and successful salespeople know this, accept this,
and work to make their chosen job sustainable. Great salespeople
are pragmatists – they want the maximum return for the
minimum effort – but they can also be rather disorganized. (Ask
any sales administrator or lawyer who has to support them.)

To manage your energy, you need a plan more than you need a
can of energy drink. Most salespeople facing a target immediately
think 'Which client will buy this amount of business from us?'
The answer they want is 'Barclays Bank', but in reality large
targets are rarely achieved with one big sale. Professional services
firms have high costs of sales because, despite – or perhaps
because of – the high fees, the average project size is always
under attack from clients. Solutions salespeople have more
chance of winning big time with the combination of technology,
software, consulting, licences and maintenance, but such sales are
lengthy processes and, as the man said, frankly tiring. You have
to work hard to understand what represents high value to this
client and how to adapt what you offer to meet this.

FOCUS YOUR EFFORT

For this to work, you will need to focus your energy. Great
salespeople are meticulous about how they prioritize the
relationships in which they invest and which tasks they prioritize.

There are only so many hours in the day and outcomes matter for salespeople as much as clients. Your number-one outcome is the deal signed in double-quick time (or to a timetable that matches your quota).

You need to prioritize your efforts in two ways:

1. Building relationships with people who are potentially important for your medium-term success as a salesperson
2. Demonstrating value to people who are moving rapidly through the funnel, because they are in a hurry and their need is urgent.

The first group will be a strategic resource; the second are your hot prospects. As the adrenalin pumps more for the hot prospect, the risk is that you will always prioritize the urgent over the important. Dealing with the urgent opportunities is not just about adrenalin; it is also about stress. Sales processes are never entirely under your control because of the way in which clients individually and collectively take decisions. You can do an all-nighter and win. You can do an all-nighter and lose. Whatever mind games you and your manager play on the team, and whatever the outcome, this is not a great way to manage energy. Big highs and big lows are exhausting in the end. People burn out.

Divide your time equally between the 'now' and 'future' prospects.

CLARIFY YOUR RELATIONSHIP-BUILDING OBJECTIVES AND CREATE A PLAN

Consider a relationship-based approach to planning. If you think like this, your plan is not just about targets but also based on progressing client relationships:

- from 'target' to 'lead'
- from 'lead' to 'prospect'
- from 'prospect' to 'buyer'
- from 'existing buyer' to 'repeat buyer'/'reference' (a client you can use for marketing)
- from 'repeat buyer' to 'advocate' (a client who does your marketing for you).

An individual client you know may start at any place on this hierarchy of customer relationships, and the first step is to categorize all your customers in this way.

Target customers may initially be sectors or organizations or possibly named individuals. Your aim is to list *names of people* as companies are only called 'clients' when used as references to other clients. LinkedIn and company websites are not bad places to start. Your aim is to research people you want to meet and who you think might have a need for a solution based on the competencies of your company.

Leads are customers with whom you have started to engage. The bottom line is to list the actions you propose taking to develop some 'hook' or discussion point that will pique their curiosity to get you in front of the targeted individual. This is often time-consuming, as you and the team are doing a lot of research and also listening to the client. You will also have some clients who are 'stuck' at this stage; you meet periodically but you have never got further than a polite chat and then the brush-off. For them, the planned actions may need to be rather more direct and challenging to ascertain whether there *is* any need you can help with, and, if this is not going to be the case – they have just signed a five-year deal with a major competitor – to stop investing in this relationship for the time being.

Prospects are people you have met who have an identified need that you can sell to. This is more than interest, this is a potential project, service or solution, but when you first put somebody on this list you do not know whether or not they have the influence, budget or support to make a decision. For most solutions, multiple stakeholders will also be involved. For the prospects, most of your actions will be about identifying them as potential decision-makers and, if they turn out to be duds, following up with other stakeholders who might become your main focus instead. Once people are identified as prospects, you usually have to include them in your lead tracking system as they represent your company's forward order book. Salespeople are cautious about raising their expectations too soon. This whole stage also includes drafting proposals, negotiating and getting legal contracts signed – in fact, anything that moves the client from seeing a possibility to signing the deal.

Buyers also need the salesperson's attention in the solutions world. In the product world, once the client had signed, the salesperson was free to move on to the next lead or prospect, but now clients expect some continuity of service from the person who secured the deal as well as the delivery manager. For some organizations this is new territory; follow-on business is prospected by the delivery manager and then the salesperson gets involved. If the idea of lifetime relationship means anything, salespeople have to check that the promise they made is being met. So actions on the buyer section of the plan include quality-assuring the implementation, helping to resolve the inevitable problems that arise and generally digging about for additions to the contract or extensions to the work.

Repeat buyers are important to nurture, as they are more significant as references than one-time-only customers. The people on this part of your plan may have been loyal repeatedly or several times over the years with fallow periods of no purchases; this will depend on what your company sells and how far your company competencies have created solutions for both growth and the downturn. Actions with these clients will include introducing other salespeople for the cross-sell or upsell possibilities, stimulus activity such as invitations to marketing events and demos, and relationship maintenance actions such as social events.

Advocates are the repeat buyers who spontaneously refer you to their friends at the gym or professional association. These clients are more likely to be your longer-standing relationships where the personal rapport has gone beyond being based on some common ground and reliability. The relationship may even be socially close – joint family holidays, for example – and so much of the activity is not just work-related; it is also focused on moving the relationship of trust to a deeper level when your relative roles (customer–salesperson) are less important than your human connection.

Planning in this way complements the more analytical approach of chunking down a sales target.

ALLOW YOURSELF SOME DOWNTIME

It is hard to allow yourself time off if the targets are not being achieved. There is stress from your manager, and from yourself. You seem to be spending all the time at work and not recharging your batteries.

Achieving a good balance is a skill:

'I break down my target by quarters and consider what leads, prospects and qualified prospects I have. If the picture looks bad, I know I will need to target other people, but I don't panic; I always do some prospecting, even if the funnel looks positive. Better to have too many than too few. But I keep one evening a week and every weekend sacrosanct. You are doing this for the family in the end and if you don't have a relationship with them, what's the point? When I started out I was terrible at saying no to any meeting, but I've learned to not always be quite so available. There's a lot of "presentism" in our office and I just ignore it.'

'I'm a target-driven person. I'm training for a triathlon at the moment and I make this a priority. The danger is that all your time is spent at work or socializing with clients and this isn't healthy in our business. Setting yourself targets for lots of aspects of your life works well for me.'

Putting it all together

You won't be much use to your clients or your company if you run out of gas and there is nobody who can decide to recharge apart from you. Selling takes effort, and a plan for relationships – and for developing some aspect of you – may help you to achieve a better balance.

38 PATIENCE PAYS

*'Dripping water hollows out stone, not through force,
but persistence.'*

Ovid

Enthusiasm in most large companies is in short supply. All large
organizations tend to entropy and sclerosis because the effort
to move them is so great. The clients in them grow apathetic
and cynical. Head-on confrontation is unlikely to prevail, as the
ineluctable force encounters the immoveable object. A more Zen-
like approach is often needed.

Persistence is intrinsically attractive. Energy overcomes sclerosis,
just as optimism overcomes entropy's first cousin, cynicism. It
doesn't feel easy when you are the one knocking on the doors
that are locked and kissing the frogs that remain amphibians, but
in the end the refreshing sight of someone who seems genuinely
interested in bringing about a beneficial change may prevail.

KNOW THAT PERSISTENCE NEEDS A PROCESS

Being organized goes hand in hand with being persistent.
Introverts are generally more persistent than extroverts (who
get distracted by the next shiny thing). But salespeople tend to
be extroverted because the job needs people who are stimulated
by both relationships and external challenges and like to be in
charge of situations. Opportunism is crucially important, but so
is the ability to use your intuition about somebody and cultivate
that relationship in the medium term.

The simplest process to help you become more persistent is the
list, linked to your diary. Successful salespeople are – contrary to
perceptions – methodical. Contacting a client at regular intervals
is the norm for maintaining your client base. These contacts will

vary in time/cost, depending on the importance of that person, but clients know exactly how you value them by the frequency and nature of your contact. A quarterly email is different from your repeated efforts to get them to come to lunch with a great thinker they would enjoy meeting. The list is therefore about whom you will contact and what you will suggest to further the dialogue.

The first priority for persistence should be existing clients who have other potential needs in the short term. Assuming they are pleased with what they have bought, you are further down the funnel of sales with them than with new clients, and are more likely to close in the short term. You have a track record and you have a legitimate subject to talk about – the current delivery of the service. Their assistant has your phone number. All you have to do is identify the next need. If they are regular buyers, so much the better. Even if they aren't the biggest spenders – which they often are not – all successful salespeople know that they need to maintain what they have before building something new.

Sound dull? Farming never had the adrenalin of hunting; it takes patience watching things grow, but it is the foundation of a successful sales career.

These clients may not, of course, be the most valuable prospects in the medium term; there might be a large opportunity that is quietly bubbling away but doesn't seem to have a timetable you can really influence. These should be your second priority – important prospects that need attention. Your aim is to increase the probability of this sale happening in the foreseeable future.

The third group for your list will be clients – dormant, live or still just targets – who represent tomorrow's lunch. These are the individuals upon whose success yours relies in the medium to longer term. They are possibly more valuable than the second group, and you may have to restrict the number of these who you can actively manage over a long period of time. Bob Howe, who founded the IBM consulting group, used to say, 'You can only manage six to eight clients properly at one time', and then he would add, 'so they had better be big hitters.' These clients are those who will make your name if you can succeed with them over time.

The list is therefore divided into clients in each of these three categories and your time is divided roughly 40/25/25. The extra 10 per cent is reserved for the 'bluebirds' – those leads that appear out of a clear blue sky and want to close in the short term because somebody has recommended your company so strongly.

UNDERSTAND THAT MANY CLIENTS NEED YOUR PATIENCE

Many salespeople don't like to wait because they fear clients will change their minds, decide to do nothing, go out to tender or do anything else to delay closing the deal.

Are these anxieties real? A really big deal, such as outsourcing, cannot be taken by most customers to a timetable that works for the provider. It is a complex, strategic decision with enormous consequences for the client company and the clients themselves. Major shareholders may have a view. Staff may even lose their jobs. Deciding that something is right to do and deciding to do it now are two different things. Forcing the issue with discounts or other levers of a swift decision only cheapens your offer, even if your business needs the sale to keep people gainfully employed.

Sales managers often appear impervious to the idea that the salesperson cannot deliver the deal to a timetable they define. Depending on their own experience, this can be bravado or ignorance; first sales with new clients can take up to 18 months and really big deals can take years to come to fruition. It can test the depth of your pockets as the vendor. As one successful seller in the professional services arena said, 'Stay in the game. Your goal is not to be deselected.'

BE CLEAR WHEN YOU ARE CONSIDERING GIVING UP ON A CLIENT

This might sound contradictory, but all good salespeople sometimes 'sack' clients. Common reasons are:

- too many 'fishing trips' and not enough real opportunities
- a client who increasingly 'cherry-picks' parts of the offer – often the pieces with the lowest margin or the greatest risk to the vendor
- clients who are extremely difficult to do business with – either personally (rude and unreasonable, rather than demanding) or in terms of the way they pay (or don't).

Good clients deserve patience, but bad ones deserve honesty in terms of the impact of their behaviour on the trading relationship. People will behave as badly as we let them, because bad behaviour as a client is easiest and they can exonerate themselves because 'we are paying you guys a lot of money'.

The real point is that your company is creating great value for the customer and this value creation is put at risk by the way they are behaving. At some point, their value as a revenue generator has to be set against their costs to your staff retention and maybe your reputation in the market. Bad behaviour is most common in commodity-supplier relationships so, by definition, if you are a high-end brand and your clients start to treat you like the caterers then your positioning has slipped.

But – and this is a big but – you should never become impatient with a client without discussing the cause of your impatience. Often, we make erroneous assumptions based on limited information and even raising the issue will cause the client to disclose issues they are facing which we were unaware of: reduced budget, illness, boss under threat lashing out at his subordinates and so on. The end result is still the same; your ability as a company to create value for the client is being reduced and this concerns you in the short term – for them – and in the longer term for your own reputation.

Putting it all together

Persistence and patience are part of the successful salesperson's lot. If you lack 'stickability' in terms of relationships with often quite needy people, you may not find this aspect of the job that easy. It is particularly hard when the client's circumstances make a neat timetable in the sales funnel hard to follow. Just as your behaviour in the sales process communicates what your company will be like as deliverers, so the client's behaviour in that process is indicative of their future behaviour.

39 TWO EARS (AGAIN)

> *'Search others for their virtues.'*
> Benjamin Franklin

As you get to know the client better, you realize that the person you are working with is more human (i.e. flawed) and less robust than they seemed on first acquaintance. Your ability to listen affects your ability to ask better questions, which provoke more thoughtful answers, which produce in turn things that are more engaging to listen to.

REMEMBER THAT LISTENING IS NOT LIKE SPEAKING

Salespeople are task-oriented and target-driven. The great ones don't just say 'People buy from people'; they actually behave as if this were true. In other words, they do not make 'relating to their clients' another 'to do' on a long list of actions they need to carry out to achieve their target. They recognize that relating is not about *doing* anything, except listening – not just listening for *what* the client is saying but listening to the client as a person. This means listening not just for your own advantage as the salesperson but also listening to understand emotions, aspirations, motivations and anxieties.

The economist Otto Scharmer identifies different levels of listening and compares them to their impact on the person being listened to. Paraphrasing his insights, the first three levels could be called:

1. **listening against** – listening for what matches what you want or hope to hear
2. **listening for** – listening curiously for what surprises you by not being what you expect

3. **listening as if** – listening empathically, standing in their shoes, to understand emotional aspects, which may be stated or unstated in what the speaker says.

Salespeople tend to listen 'against' most of the time; waiting for objections and buying signals are both examples of how some salespeople are trained to do this. It helps you to control the sale. They have considered likely objections and have words to handle them. The task is to find the opportunity to say their piece. While you would describe this as listening, clients might experience it as that you were waiting to speak. The impact on the other person is that you are doing your job as salesperson but not relating to them. Listening against reinforces perceptions of the transactional nature of the relationship between the seller and the buyer.

Occasionally, you will find yourself surprised by something the client says. You lapse into 'listening for'. Your curiosity is pricked. You ask several questions for clarification, which communicates this curiosity. The client feels your curiosity in the way you ask the question; it isn't just an attempt to gain information for personal gain in the battle to promote their deal but feels different, as if you were genuinely interested in their perspective. The impact of curious listening – and curious questioning – is that it takes both the client and the salesperson in a direction that may be unfamiliar to either or both. New things might happen. It's suddenly a bit of an adventure where unknown territory may be traversed, with some potential risks on both sides, such as looking foolish or not knowing the answer. This is risky, but exciting as well.

When I have been the buyer of services, I have rarely encountered salespeople who can really do the third level – empathic listening – authentically. Many are trained to make the right noises: 'That sounds pretty challenging. Is it?' or – my personal pet peeve, beloved of journalists – 'How did that make you feel?' This kind of reaction to my answer shows that this is still transactional; there is no compassion for what I have said and little follow-up or sharing of their own feelings or experiences. I feel sceptical, not understood. Like the too-early use of a first name or the presumptive use of physical contact, attempts at empathic behaviour without judgement or reciprocation often backfire and are just intrusive.

REALIZE THAT EMPATHY STARTS WITH SELF-AWARENESS

Can you develop genuine empathy for clients? Can you make your listening to what they say genuinely 'listening with'?

While empathy is a psychological disposition – agreeableness, as it is called – which can be measured, salespeople can learn to see that real engagement through listening is a huge benefit to both parties and that genuinely working with emotion is a skill you can learn.

It starts with increasing your own awareness of how you feel when you experience listening at the deeper levels. People who are less naturally agreeable often do not really know how they themselves are feeling. You may notice this because they often have a poorly developed vocabulary for talking about emotion. So when they want to listen to clients at the deeper levels, they may not be aware that their own state of mind – for example, how tired they are feeling – will affect their ability to do this well. Empathic listening takes effort and exhausts you, possibly more than other sorts of listening; you will have to concentrate on understanding your own feelings and then putting them on the back burner to concentrate on the client as a person, a fellow human being, and not just as a client.

Why would you bother? Clients' feelings are often closely related to what they value. An area of anxiety removed might be more valuable than a gain to the bottom line. The hope of a more purposeful role in the company might be worth more to them than hitting their cost-reduction target. The passionate desire to get their idea accepted more broadly could count for more than an increase in unit productivity. Without empathy – without listening – these factors could be missed and your pitch to them might all be couched in terms of the transactional, material and task-related benefits of your solution.

LONGER TERM, CREATE TRANSFORMATIONAL OPPORTUNITIES WITH CLIENTS

The real win from profound listening is that it opens up the possibility of clients talking about ideas, dreams and all the craziness that leads to large, strategic opportunities for salespeople. If the client knows you will listen – and ask questions – without immediately either providing answers or 'selling', they begin to share half-formed notions.

Scharmer's fourth level of listening is foreign territory to both you and them. You are – as one salesperson called it – 'riffing with the client'; this is a sort of creative improvisation based on knowing each other's areas of expertise and skill, which may lead nowhere or to somewhere extraordinary. Transformation in organizations tends to start in the head of somebody. To be present at the start of this process with your client allows you unprecedented access to them and their people. It means that you are in at the ground floor of the thinking in the business about some potential future scenario, with potential consequences (maybe) for your company as well.

Of course, you can blow it. Try to turn this into an opportunity too soon and you will suddenly start 'listening against' and the client will clam up. A moment ago you were no longer the salesperson, just somebody who was helping. That useful sounding board has turned into the panel of judges and the client's little newborn, feeble idea is in danger of being strangled at birth. So, as with all sorts of trusting relationship, this level of listening can take you to places you might not really want to go. Imagine telling your boss how you spent the afternoon 'riffing with the client'. Reaction? 'You have a sales target to reach this month, let me remind you!'

Putting it all together

Longer-term authentic relationships require a less transactional approach to listening and something more like the way you would listen to a close friend: listening without an immediate purpose other than to help. Empathic and creative listening are not always easy for everybody to master, as to some extent they may be determined by factors of personality.

But if you want to provide longer-term support for your client, some of the convenient boundaries suggested by role titles like 'client' and 'sales rep' have to be superseded. Listen again and see where this leads.

40 JUDGING THE CLIENT NEVER HELPS

'Seek first to understand and then to be understood.'
Stephen Covey

Let's face it, we are all flawed. In some area or other we are all fools, dreamers, or neurotic in our different little ways. We don't mean to be. We come to work to do the best we can. We long for recognition and genuine appreciation, the warmth of others' approval. We have highly sensitive antennae for other people's arrogance, superiority and disparagement.

When you meet clients for the first time, the dominant emotion in the room is vulnerability. If they have invited you in, they are possibly feeling that they are underperforming or even failing, or at risk of doing so. If you have navigated your way to their door, you are expecting to be judged as a potential supplier of services or support and, although seasoned salespeople describe this as an 'adrenalin rush', you know one potential outcome is failure and that you may never meet this person again.

This shared vulnerability has odd consequences. Both parties will tend to be rather more aggressive and 'show off' more than they need to. Both parties will act as if the outcome of this meeting isn't really that important – a sort of fake insouciance about the problem. Both parties will be super-sensitive about anything that might be interpreted as an attack or a criticism. If it sounds a bit like a first date, it is.

Extrinsic factors may increase the client's sense of vulnerability:

- Their boss suggested they talk with you (or, worse still, the boss's boss).
- Personally, they didn't want to consult advisers/providers, they wanted to handle the matter themselves, but everybody else in their department insisted.
- This is the first time they have held a job at this level, or dealt with solution providers or...

At the same time, as a sales professional you know you have to put on a good show, to impress the client enough to get a second chance. If you are totally unchallenging, this is unlikely to happen. So you need to choose your moment to shine. As the client holds the social advantage in this situation – they are doing *you* the favour – you usually wait for their signal to talk or ask questions. When the agenda is unclear to both, this awkwardness can last a few moments. If you haven't agreed the objectives of the meeting before it starts, chances are the client will suddenly say 'OK, tell me what you provide', or something similar. This is not what you wanted, as 'Telling isn't selling'. You wanted an exchange of information – a dialogue, not a soliloquy.

So you may fall for presenting your solution long before you should, and those slides that your manager said should never come out of your bag do, and you can see her eyes glazing over after the first slide and you are... doomed. Judged and found wanting. Vulnerability has led you to do what door-to-door salespeople do and which doesn't work with B2B selling.... Successful salespeople don't start with a pitch. Successful salespeople prevent the vulnerability from leading them into this trap.

ESTABLISH THE AGENDA BEFORE YOU START

'Dear Caroline, Thanks for agreeing to see me next week. John [the intermediary] thought you would be interested in discussing the work we have been doing on [name issue you are using as a starting point] and considering any implications for you and your company. Of course I would like to learn more about your situation and whether any of the skills and experience we have could be useful to you. Is there anything particular you would like me to prepare before we meet?'

'Dear Jack, That sounds fine. I'll have about 40 minutes. I'd be interested in anything you have which would help me compare our company with the industry as a whole in respect of [issue already raised]. See you next Tuesday.'

Is this an agenda? Not quite, but it means that you can cut to the chase when you meet and agree to spend 20 minutes on their situation and 20 minutes on your bait. This will get over some of the vulnerability about how to play it and you will already be working *with* your client, not as a supplicant at their shrine. When you meet, after the usual pleasantries, you can then lead with a confirmation of that agenda and get on with the conversation. With any luck, you will start with the lead and her situation and then be able to tailor what you have brought to match what you have heard.

ASK PERMISSION BEFORE YOU CHALLENGE

The tacit 'rule' for first meetings is that both parties are seeking to understand, not to criticize. Astonishing numbers of salespeople get this wrong, feeling that in response to the brief the client has sent out, or other information they have been given, they must point out to the client the error of their ways. If they don't, they are not 'challenging' enough and legend has it that clients expect to be challenged. 'I'm not sure you have a really robust strategy behind what you have asked us to pitch for.' 'It seems that the real commercial backing for this decision hasn't been completely worked out.' 'Your competitors would smile if they knew this was what you were considering.' These astonishing words are real examples from my time as a client. The intention might have been to provide a useful critique but the unintended consequence was rudeness.

The reality is that clients *like* their thinking to be challenged, but only on their terms and when their status as top dog is clear. The alternative favoured by successful salespeople is a three-stage process:

1. Listen and ask questions for clarification about their issue. Summarize your understanding.
2. Ask the client if they would like to hear an outsider's initial view. (Usually they say yes, as they have agreed to see you. If they don't, you haven't listened well enough or long enough to have earned a hearing, so ask more questions.)
3. If they agree, comment favourably on two elements of their situation/action, and critically on two others, in that order.

The client has retained control because you asked permission. Your criticism is balanced. Their vulnerability has not increased. They may even be feeling slightly relieved, having shared information with somebody who might be able to help. The time for your more trenchant challenges is not now. Later, when they trust you more, they will welcome your more robust critique and you will have the chance to 'educate' them.

EMPATHIZE WITH THE CLIENT

Clients often seek confirmation from the outsider. This is a good sign that they see you as somebody with authority, but it can be difficult to handle.

The client may ask, 'So, based on what I've told you, what do you think? Was there anything we missed?' The answer they want is a resounding 'No', but you must be careful not to fall into the trap of letting them off the hook when you know little of the situation – apart from what they have told you – and nothing much about the alternatives.

So you play safe and empathize with them and their situation. If they are seeking reassurance from a near stranger, they are feeling pretty sensitive. 'I'm not sure about things you missed, but I'd have found that pretty difficult. How did you feel about the decision?'

Now they can talk about the emotional and political elements, which may be part of their vulnerability as much as the commercial decision. You can continue to empathize: 'Was it stressful? Not just you. Other people? What do you feel about it now, with hindsight? What do you feel about your own question – if something was missed?' Now you can chance giving an opinion on the original question, if you have one: 'When these things don't turn out as promised, there are always things we could have done or said. The bigger question is usually one of [e.g. data; link to your solution/service]. Did you have the right sort of [e.g. data] to hand to decide which option was best?'

Finally, don't rubbish them afterwards if you fail to get what you want. It isn't *their* fault that your chemistry was wrong, your ideas were unsuitable, your explanations faulty. 'They didn't understand the technology. Sigh. They were never going to be early adopters – sigh.' If you pin the blame on the client, you may be failing to learn important lessons about your ability to communicate, listen or sell.

Putting it all together

As a partner in a professional services firm expressed it:

'If I hear someone slagging off a client, I know that they have failed and they want to hide it. But it doesn't work. The client is misguided, the client makes a mistake; thank God, it provides the rationale for our business. That's why they need our help. Our job is to accept clients for what they are and to help them improve their business as best we can, even when, if we were to meet them in the pub, we would walk away. Professional relationships are not pub relationships.'

Worst of all is judging your client to be a fool. This says everything about you and nothing about them.

41 TRUST IS A TWO-WAY STREET

'Mankind has little need for truth, but a very strong need for certainty.'

Claude LeBon

B2B salespeople talk about trust more than any other thing, except winning. It's their holy grail, a deep and trusting relationship with somebody who buys when they need them to. Often, they say things like, 'Wouldn't it be great to be able to accelerate the process of building trust?' or 'How can you get the customer to trust what you say as quickly as possible, so that you can close the deal, even if the details remain a bit sketchy?'

Think about that notion. Think about what it really means in relationship terms. If greater trust is only a means to *your* end, then, as the salesperson, you are a manipulative, disrespectful, callous human being and not worthy of the customer's trust in the first place. You are conforming to the stereotype of the fairground barker promising the undeliverable miracle inside the tent. You may be amusing but hardly someone to do business with in the longer term.

So what is a different, more productive way for salespeople to think about building 'trust'? You are *not* talking about bonding with this person so that you get to be the maid of honour at their wedding or the person they turn to when they are down on their luck again (although this might happen... unintentionally). You are *not* talking about being trusted in the same way as a close friend or life partner trusts you. You are *not* talking about trust as a currency to be cashed in for personal gain. You are talking about creating sufficient mutual empathy in the relationship for both parties to give each other real, useful information around which you can agree a trade, and even perhaps a series of trades, in the years to come.

Trust cannot be forced because it is, as a very successful saleswoman told me, a two-way street. Trust is a function of personality – some people give their trust more easily than others – but you can affect the rate at which people will trust you, up to a point. Everybody has a limit to the number of people they would trust absolutely. For many it is a very short list. Trading becomes inherently suspect if the relationship is transactional. If you are the only chemist's shop for 200 miles and I need your advice about what I should take, you will not try to sell me something expensive and useless, no matter how bad the takings have been last week. Because if you do I will not just complain to you, I will tell everybody in the community that you tried to con me. Breaking trust – even though I, the customer, have no other option but to take your advice – in this situation is commercial suicide.

The Internet has made the world into a community of information about the performance of almost every product, service and vendor on the planet, so your company is now just like that chemist's shop. The opportunities for avoiding the consequences of broken trust are very, very few. Bad products being 'dumped' in developing markets? Poor delivery record? Dodgy employment practices when your staff join the outsourcing company? If customers have access to the Internet, they will probably find out.

Online reviews are the second most trusted source of information about products, second only to family and friends:

- In a Nielsen survey of 28,000 Internet users in 56 countries, 70 per cent of respondents indicated that they trust messages from this source 'completely' or 'somewhat'.
- In the US, 30 per cent of consumers start their only purchase research with Amazon, which with its wealth of reviews has become a clearing house for product information.
- A McKinsey report found that more than 60 per cent of consumers of facial skincare products go online to conduct further research *after* they have made the purchase.

It is only a matter of time before all solutions and solutions providers are subject to the same scrutiny as an eBay seller or a TripAdvisor hotel.

So trust has moved from becoming a choice between two people (hard to enforce or monitor) to being a tactic between two companies (which will be monitored and reported upon) to achieve better value from trading for both parties. The aim of trust in selling is a win–win result, not crude advantage for one party over the other.

BE CLEAR ABOUT WHERE THE STREET STARTS...

'Two way' means that there must be reciprocity about the different elements of trust:

- Chemistry – you and the person you are dealing with must find enough in common for the relationship to have a future
- Credibility – mutual respect based on an appreciation of each other's knowledge, experience or skill (or all three)
- Commitment – a readiness on both sides to deliver what you say you will
- Risk – an equal appetite for the inevitable risks involved in achieving the sponsor's desired outcome.

Once you are aware of these elements in the process of selling, you can work on them. Inauthentic behaviour and unrealistic promises do not work in building trust. Looking at this list, you can see why.

USE BEHAVIOURS ASSOCIATED WITH DEEPENING TRUST

You cannot impose your wish to build trust on another person. If the client has recently had a bad experience at work – being fired, say – then this recent major disaster will affect how far they trust anybody, so you usually have to move at the pace which both of you are comfortable with.

It starts with the first contact. If you are a natural extrovert, you will have advantages here in that people will see you as 'open', ' easy to read' and probably friendly, whether they are introverted or extroverted themselves. When, however, you move to the next level – finding some common interest, experience or relationships – similarity is reassuring, so being *too* extroverted or *too* introverted may become a problem. The emotionally intelligent salesperson will 'read' their client's behaviour and adapt to what they see, to reflect the personality of the client in front of them.

Studies in service environments have shown that demonstrating understanding of what the client says may be more important than either matching language or mirroring behaviour. Waiters taking orders where they repeat what the customers have asked for *in their own words* get substantially bigger tips. In the retail environment this careful repetition of the customer's words also increases the likelihood of sales by 10 per cent, unless it is perceived as mimicry. In proposal writing, successful partners often advise the use of the client's own words to describe either their objectives or valued outcomes from the project.

More real than repetition for understanding is the discovery of shared goals. One successful salesperson I interviewed said that what he brought to the table was a hunger for change and innovation, a real dedication to commercial outcomes and a genuine pride in what his company delivered. When qualifying clients, he was looking for the same things as indicators that this person would be a 'good' client. The common ground was therefore aspiration for improvement and growth, something many clients would respond to. If he didn't see these aspirations in the client, then he invested less.

Empathizing takes time. Many of the people you meet are very busy and, although they like to talk and be heard as much as the salesperson, they are often rapid decision-makers, who need to qualify you as potentially useful as much as you need to qualify them. This slightly strange paradox – how to develop empathy when there is no time – can sometimes be helped by moving the conversation from enquiry to dialogue. Experienced salespeople say you should invite questions from your clients as soon as possible. Putting yourself up for cross-examination may feel risky, but is actually the best way to qualify them, just as the questions you ask will probably be the best way for a customer to qualify *you*.

WRITE FINAL PROPOSALS WHEN YOU TRUST EACH ANOTHER

In most complex solutions and B2B service selling there are gaps in what exactly you can promise your customer and both parties know that these gaps exist. In other words, there will always be a moment when the seller will have to say – in a trusting relationship – 'We don't exactly know the answer to that now, but it will be OK.' For the seller, this is where the trust you have built up pays you back. For the customer, this is where they recognize that anything worth having will always involve a certain amount of risk and they are glad that this person opposite is on their side to help.

You can ask broad empathy questions to establish some of this:

- 'Are you happy with where we have got to?'
- 'And others? How are they feeling about doing this?'
- 'What else might we have to do to get this understood?'
- '... and accepted?'
- '... and actually made to happen?'

Also consider what your answer would be to the same questions. Sometimes it pays to reflect on this with the customer:

- 'I'm not sure how committed you feel to what we have been discussing. Can you let me know where you are about all this?'
- 'Let's just take a minute to put our cards on the table. I'm happy to go first. I think I've made a good case for what we can offer and I think you are persuaded about the commercial value of this. I think you are still rather uncertain about doing business with me and I don't want this to be an issue for the deal, which is in both our company's best interests. What about you?'
- 'I'm starting to feel excited about this project. But I'm not getting much sense of what you feel about it all. Can you tell me?'

Putting it all together

Business-to-business deals are about making one plus one equal three. If the relationship is an impediment to this calculus from either side, then this should be worked on and worked through. This requires courage on both sides, as aspects like trust and emotions generally are much harder for many people to talk about than the nuts and bolts of the deal. But they are just as real.

*'The US culture is strongly built on the tacit assumption of
pragmatism, individualism and status through achievement.
These assumptions introduce a strong bias for getting the job
done, which, combined with individualism, leads to a devaluing
of relationship building, teamwork and collaboration except as
a means to the end of task accomplishment.'*
                                                    Ed Schein

Everybody remembers the time they got culture a bit wrong...

'This was a meeting I will never forget. It's a long time ago
now. China. Just after Nixon seemed to open things up. Two
of us Americans were going to a meeting with Party officials
to pitch building a factory as a joint venture. We were green,
but keen. We knew there would be a committee and when the
two of us and the interpreter arrived at the enormous party
headquarters building, we weren't really that hopeful.

'We were shown into a large rectangular room with pictures
of Chairman Mao on one wall between the windows and the
largest red curtain I've ever seen covering the other. Or that's
what we thought. There were two chairs in the middle of the
room – and another for the interpreter. Opposite, a long table
with about 20 chairs on the side facing us, and then two more
rows behind. It looked a though their delegation was about
50–60 people. We sat down and they all filed in. The head of the
Party delegation has his interpreter, too. (Turns out he speaks
perfect English anyway.) Through the interpreter, he welcomes
us and then asks "Would you mind if this meeting is observed?"

'Facing the 60 of them, we didn't have much choice. "Sure,
OK," we say. He waves his hand and the red curtain begins
to draw back. Behind it were ranks and ranks of young
Chinese on what looked like the stands you see at sporting

events – 400, maybe 500 people. We were really taken aback. "What are they here for?" my colleague stuttered. The head of the delegation said something to the interpreter. She smiled sweetly. "Sorry. They are here to learn.'"

If you work in teams comprising people from different cultures or selling into a different culture from your own, you need to take advice about how buying and selling work in that culture and never assume that the people in that culture are like you. This advice might relate to things like:

• which of your brand values are likely to be appreciated more
• how to approach a senior person
• how decisions are made in this environment.

In Europe you will find wide diversity of approaches to these aspects of selling. Managing the cultural trip wires is a lifelong study, according to great salespeople.

Environments that are less ethnically diverse than major cities have distinctive behaviours, attitudes, values and beliefs. Successful salespeople consider the impact of these differences on their assumptions about how to behave and what to expect in a sales cycle within a different culture.

Take authority. Power in organizations is influenced by the culture of the company and often its origins in a specific nation. Geert Hoftstede conducted a much-quoted piece of research for IBM in the 1980s to assess whether there were such things as national cultural differences. His heroic project identified a range of cultural 'indices', one of which is particularly relevant to dealing with stakeholders in different cultures. He called it 'power distance', which he defined as 'the extent to which the less powerful members of institutions and organizations within a country expect and accept that power is distributed unequally'. In countries of high power distance, superiors and subordinates both see each other as beings 'of a different kind': powerful people emphasize their power in the way they present themselves; older people are respected; and the way to change the system is by dethroning people in power. In countries with low power distance, inequality should be minimized: subordinates and superiors are just people like us; people should have equal rights; age does not imply respect; and the way to change things is to redistribute power. Using research from many sources, he then ranked countries around the world. Countries like Malaysia, Guatemala, the Philippines, Mexico and the Arab countries were all high on this index; Austria, Israel, New Zealand and the Scandinavian countries were ranked low, as was the UK.

Although Hoftstede's ideas have since been contested and the research predates the Internet, the idea that authority manifests itself differently around the world rings true to anyone who has tried to do business on different continents. You see it in who has to sponsor the purchase of the solution, how change is envisaged and the way in which implementation takes place. You also see it in the relationship that the provider has to offer the client: equal, trusted adviser, or subordinate vendor.

ALLOW TIME TO MEET, TALK AND DECIDE

Consider the time it takes to make a sale. A northern European or US reader of this book will have a linear sense of time. You will plan your sales and your diary and try to fit in what you can into your day. You will be expected to account for your time to your boss because, in your way of thinking, time is money. If decisions aren't made to a schedule you are wasting time, so if your client isn't deciding on time you must be doing something wrong. If you waste your client's time, you can expect to fail.

This is not so if you are working in southern Europe where, according to Richard Lewis, societies are multi-active rather than linear-active in their relationship to time. They are not interested in schedules and deadlines; they want to fit as much activity as they can into their day. This means they pay more attention to what is happening now than to the consequences. For example, they would rather complete a conversation with you and keep somebody else waiting if the conversation is stimulating. Arabs, Italians, Spaniards and Greeks are all more interested in face time than punctuality, because this secures the relationship with the person they are with. Cancellation is just postponement so, when you meet them, notice how much time they give you; it is indicative of how they value the relationship.

The third option is cyclic time, which is the way some Eastern cultures see things. (Don't generalize too much about 'Asia', however.) Time is not in short supply, but the past dictates what you can do in the present because there will be another cycle, and the customer's actions today will influence the next cycle. This means that the customer must be circumspect and allow enough time to pass for the best approach to make itself known to them. Prioritization is not a controlled, rational process but a gradual revelation. The linear-active way to make decisions is to balance the pros and cons of each alternative in turn; the multi-active way would be to discuss the options fully until the consensus emerges.

In places like Thailand, where the cycle of the seasons is more real than the deadline, haste does not make much sense. Chinese people share this idea but are also aware of the value of time, so expect punctuality; salespeople working in China often remark on how the Chinese customer expects to spend far longer getting to know somebody than we do in the West. Once this time has been invested, then the dealing can start. Japanese customers expect their salespeople to respect the proper divisions of time: a couple of minutes to exchange business cards at the start of the meeting, an invitation from your customer to start the business discussion, a suitable period at the end for gratitude to be expressed. Doing business here is another ritual and must be done properly, with respect for tradition.

Tourism, international work experience and the Internet may gradually erode these different attitudes to time and the behaviours they engender, but their basis is rooted in thousands of years of culture. The fundamental lesson for salespeople from the linear-active cultures to learn is patience; relationships and revelations take time.

RECOGNIZE THE NEED TO MAKE A CONSULTATIVE DECISION

When it comes to deciding to buy or the scope of the service requirement, culture also has a part to play. In particular, the role of individualism versus collectivism determines what 'good' decisions look like. According to Hofstede, the US leads the way on individualism followed by other English-speaking countries – Australia, the UK, Canada and New Zealand – and the Netherlands. In these environments, decisions are often delegated to the appropriate individual, although if the culture is also low on power distance, that person may have to persuade others of the legitimacy of their decision. In Denmark, New Zealand, the US and the UK (individualistic and low power distance cultures), you might need to help your client to sell the idea inside the company.

Collectivist cultures include many countries in Central and South America, as well as Korea, Taiwan, Singapore and Hong Kong. Many of these countries are also high on power distance, which suggests that decision-making is likely to be made by groups of senior people, often without reference to the needs or wishes of their subordinates. Selling into this culture requires you to be seen as part of that elite and for you to persuade the senior group of the value of the proposition you are selling.

All such ideas come with a big health warning about quick 'answers'. Any stereotyping may lead to the wrong tactics and create barriers to trust. You may be selling to a person of Chinese parentage, brought up and educated in Australia but working for a French company. However, in the global marketplace, customers are increasingly expecting responses to be tailored to them as individuals and in a way that reflects the culture of their organization.

REMEMBER THAT CLIENTS NEED TO LOOK GOOD

Most people's sales experience teaches them that the rule of 'making your client look good' is universal. What this means, however, may vary from one culture to another. Consider your last sale into another culture. Did 'making your client look good' mean:

- making him look more powerful?
- making her look clever?
- making him look tough and decisive?
- making her look collegial and collaborative?

or some blend of all these?

You might also consider the opposite. Would 'making your client look bad' mean:

- diminishing her authority in the eyes of her peers?
- making him look foolish or stupid?
- making him look weak and indecisive?
- making her look aggressive and overly competitive with her colleagues?

If you ask yourself these questions, you soon discover that there is no simple answer and that the best way to think about this is usually a mix of company culture and personality.

Putting it all together

Whatever you think about the specifics of these attempts to frame culture to enable us to predict how certain aspects of a sale might run, there is no doubt that every sales process encounters some aspects of culture 'clash'. Doing business with a law firm is not like doing business with a high-tech start-up in terms of expectations. Add 'Japanese' to 'law firm' and 'South African' to 'high-tech start-up' and the lessons are clear.

Much of the thinking and research about selling originates in America – a linear-active culture that is highly individualistic and medium on power distance. These attributes become assumptions, which we have to remember may not be relevant in all cultures.

'Understanding selling's social purpose as great art dealers do and enjoying its possibilities are crucial steps to becoming any good at it.'
Philip Delves Broughton

Selling is exciting but also stressful, not least because of the amount of rejection involved. Even the most successful salesperson admits to those rather bleak moments when nothing seems to be going in your direction and the competition is eating your breakfast. Great salespeople are rather like entertainers; when they come off the stage to deafening applause, they remember why they love the job. When nobody buys tickets for the show, they remember why they hate it.

The challenge is to stay positive and motivated, as these feelings influence the way you behave and your behaviour influences your chances of success. In one study, 77 per cent of salespeople said they thought attitude was more important to sales success than skill. Research supports the notion that optimists sell more: in a study of life insurance – which has the highest rate of rejection of any type of selling – the most optimistic salespeople sold up to 88 per cent more than their more pessimistic colleagues.

Fitness in selling, as the person who suggested this to me pointed out, is about more than just attitude; it is an approach to manage body, mind and spirit. If you are physically fit, you feel more confident; research indicates this has slightly more impact on women's performance and earnings than men's. You are also capable of sustaining your efforts over longer periods of time. You look better. The sport you practise provides you with something to talk about. It shows you are somebody who sets themselves goals and achieves them. And it doesn't have to be a triathlon to be interesting: any fitness activity says something about you and may help your client to get to know you more quickly.

How would you know you were mentally sales fit? The biggest challenge for most would be a few days on the desks, cold-calling. Most successful salespeople have got beyond this approach, although all of them have had experience of doing this. If this is your lot, here is some research to consider when planning your calls:

• The best times to call are between 8 and 9 a.m. and 4 and 5 p.m., in terms of results.
• Thursday is the best day and Friday the worst.
• Leads from your website need a response in five minutes to have any chance of becoming prospects.
• Of the clients who say they will call back, 95 per cent don't. You need to secure their commitment to taking your call.
• Motivation for disagreeable tasks follows a U-curve. People are more productive at the start and towards the end than they are in the middle, suggesting that the best prospects should be placed earlier and later in any call schedule (although this might create a self-fulfilling prophecy!).

IDENTIFY WHAT YOU ARE DOING RIGHT AND AVOID SELF-DEFEATING THINKING

There will be tasks in B2B selling which you do not relish but which you know are important. Salespeople cite different areas they tend to avoid; completing sales administration was high on the list. Others disliked attending or speaking at conferences. Identify the connection between the activity you dislike and your longer-term success, perhaps as a ratio (20 client conference speeches led to ten enquiries which became three sales?) or with a beneficial outcome (speedy client admin increased client satisfaction, particularly at the final stages of the campaign?). Knowing this may help to motivate you. Chores may be necessary steps to achieving the goal.

When things do not work out, concentrating on what worked well as well as what didn't can be useful in motivating yourself to continue. Even when you lose, invite the client to provide you with positive feedback on the calls, the proposal and the final pitch: 'What did we do right that we should build upon next time?' This emphasizes to the client that it was a close-run thing (you hope) and, over time, helps you to hone your skill.

After a series of failed bids, it is easy to feel that you are not cut out for selling or that what you sell is not competitive – or any combination of negative self-assessments. It is important to differentiate what happened from your interpretation of what happened. One salesperson, who now has a one-in-three record of success, recalls:

> 'When it goes pear-shaped, which it does, I used to criticize myself for the failure. My colleagues used to bolster me a bit, but as we were all in competition with one another it didn't take much for me to see through some of this.

> 'What I do now is different. There is a big "down" moment when the customer rings to say your bid has lost, so I accept that for the rest of that day I won't be able to do anything very positive, and occupy myself with boring tasks like completing my expenses claims or something similar. This is the acceptance piece – much better than blaming people or shouting or pretending it didn't happen. That evening I do something I might otherwise do to celebrate – like taking the kids to a movie or going out for dinner. It's a way of resetting what is, in reality, a stumble but not, ultimately, a fall.

> 'What has happened and your attitude to what has happened are not the same thing. You cannot control rejection. You can control your attitude.'

BE CREATIVE

Here are some concrete tips from successful salespeople. I can't vouch for their effectiveness but they demonstrate how creativity helps to keep you motivated:

- Buy a telephone headset and do all telephone calls standing up. This makes you feel more powerful and, by raising your status, the timbre of your voice also changes to sound more authoritative.

- Before meeting clients or speaking on the phone, sniff peppermint or drink peppermint tea, not coffee. The smell of peppermint helps with attention and alertness and lightens your mood. (Caffeine takes about 20 minutes to kick in and there are huge variations in the amount you get in an espresso.)
- If you feel negative, write down your failings on a piece of paper and either make it into a dart and send it into the bin or tear it up. One person recommends snapping a rubber band against your wrist every time you feel negative; the idea is that a painful response to a negative notion will discourage further negative notions.
- Go to the gym before the client meeting. Construct the workout so that you achieve something better than usual; the combination of success and endorphins helps before a key sales call.
- Smile. Even smiling to yourself reduces stress. Even the position of the face may help you feel better. (Putting chopsticks in your mouth was a tip somebody had picked up on a sales training course.)
- Laugh. If you are the kind of person who gives yourself a hard time, a YouTube clip of your favourite comedy helps to readjust your mood.
- If you are coming to the end of a big campaign and the stakes are high, write yourself the rejection email from the client before the pitch. Then write your reply setting out why the client's rejection is misplaced. It may help you position the pitch or final-stage meeting.

WHEN YOU FAIL, WORK OUT WHAT DID WORK

Optimists sell more than the pessimists, but they also respond to failure in a different way. A depressed salesperson tends to think, 'It's all my fault. This will never change. It's typical of the way I am.' An optimist thinks, 'This is a specific case. There's no reason to think it will continue to happen in this way. Lots of people were involved and it isn't all under our control anyway.'

What is your approach to failure? The sales-fit salesperson who tends towards the optimist's position will reflect on the case and try to work out why the team failed without getting depressed. If you have to manage the post-mortem – or are conducting one in your head – you might ask:

- What were the distinguishing features of this sales campaign/ bid?
- What did we do differently in this campaign compared to others that were similar? What worked and what didn't?
- With hindsight, what could we have done to improve our chances?
- Are there any general insights from this case that we should bear in mind in future campaigns?

These questions will throw up answers that show you controlled less of the process than you thought. The answers may also encourage you to look forward in different ways – to apply the insights, to find another opportunity on which to 'practise' and to look for positive signs of success.

Successful salespeople often say they are 'still learning how to sell'. Although not personally humble, they are often sure that they haven't got the sales process licked just yet. This makes them continuous students, even though they are also expert at what they do; they are continuously stretching their understanding at the margins of what they know how to do, using small conscious changes to add to their larger unconscious pool of competence. You are never bored then, despite the setbacks, as every review is adding to your longer-term chances of success. Look at those ratios; over time they do improve.

The final element of sales fitness is belief. What is the good that your service does? How does buying what you sell help customers? What is the moral purpose in your job? It is important to be able to look in the mirror every morning and answer these questions because the commercial value of a service without some moral purpose attached is less motivating in the longer term.

Putting it all together

Physical and mental fitness are about a disciplined approach. When managers seek to become leaders, they have to move from meeting objectives defined for them by others to defining their own agenda for change in the organization where they work. This moves them from 'just' managing tasks and teams to stimulating people to deliver exceptional effort in line with a worthwhile goal.

The same is true of successful salespeople; you are on a mission to improve the world as well as achieve a sales target. The desire to improve things is moral as well as commercial. It gives you the energy to confront complacency and 'immorality' in your customers. It is the evangelical aspect of selling which you need to keep you going, no matter how often the door is closed in your face. Keep this belief in the moral importance of what you are doing alive and the rest is easier to bear. Sales-fit beliefs are as important for sustainable success as all the rest.

44 SELLING IS A SERVICE

'Here is a simple but powerful rule: always give people more than they expect to get.'
Nelson Boswell

If your organization separates sales from delivery, then it is easy to make your own organization's convenience into a barrier for customers. For products, the separation makes sense because the production of the asset precedes the sale; but in services and solutions much of the production comes after the customer signs.

The salesperson is in effect the broker between the client's needs and the company's production capabilities. You make yourself accountable for that brokerage, working to the client's satisfaction in terms of the proposal and ultimately the delivery. This is a service you are providing and you have two sets of clients: your own company and the customer. Satisfying both is not easy, since in the product world both clients were seen in opposition to each other. It is a major test of your trustworthiness that there will have to be compromises on both sides for the sale to proceed.

As in any service relationship, customers are reassured by your ability to improvise and resolve the problems that are built into the 'one servant, two masters' situation. Consciously or unconsciously, they may test your service orientation in different ways, for example by:

- altering the timetable for bids without much notice
- bringing people you do not know to meetings without telling you
- asking for information they have already received in a different format
- calling for a meeting on a Saturday morning.

A good service provider rises to these challenges, as these are ways to communicate that their company will provide good service and this leads to more business. But the salesperson can often find themselves caught in the middle.

SHARE THE NEED TO PROVIDE GOOD SERVICE WITH OTHERS

What defines a great service relationship? Top of most customers' lists would be responsiveness – the time it takes for you to reply to that call or email, the way you arrange cover for when you go on holiday, the fact that you give them your mobile number. Responsiveness is intrusive and nobody wants to be 'always on' to a client, and when they have signed they will usually accept some rota arrangement where they get to contact a knowledgeable person when they need to.

During the sales cycle, you and the team are the customers' testing ground for this responsiveness. How do you demonstrate your commitment to improving your client's business? The first principle is that you *add value*: you deliver more than the client expects. If their previous experience of solutions salespeople has been poor, this is relatively easy, but when they are considering abandoning the market leader in favour of your company you will have to raise your game. This means:

- actively managing expectations on delivery time and quality so that you can exceed them (if the task takes the team a day, tell the client they can have it in two and then delight them by delivering a few hours early)
- providing your client with access to information they didn't expect (this works especially well when the information is transparently not about the sale but about the relationship: the details of that family hotel you discussed, a copy of a book)
- being genuinely available for clients' questions at any time (not just saying you are).

The second principle is that you consciously build up goodwill in the relationships on both sides. You need to provide your clients with a map explaining who is doing what in the bidding process and ask them to do the same. This means that you build multiple points of contact and don't get all the calls yourself. Selling solutions is a team activity because one person cannot manage all the stakeholder relationships. The brief is for people on your side to create a sense of obligation in these relationships. This is not about tickets to the final – which some organizations will not accept – but about genuinely trying to find out what the person values that your company can supply, and providing it. This might be, for example:

- access to your rather nice meeting room for an offsite
- extra copies of some document, or different versions of the document for different internal audiences
- a chance to meet and discuss issues in a social setting.

The customer will know what is going on, but this doesn't invalidate the idea that you and the team want to help and respond to them as you would in service delivery. Of course, such activity must be proportionate to the value of the sale, but *demonstrating* what they will get when they buy is far more effective than telling them.

SEE SELLING AS DIAGNOSIS

'The reason I enjoy meeting new clients is you never know what you will uncover. We are detectives, doctors and travel agents all rolled into one. Sometimes there is some anomaly in the performance of the business which they don't understand and they need us to investigate. Sometimes they have a problem, but they don't know the cause. Sometimes they know the destination, but they don't know how to get there. I use this idea of who I am and what I do a lot when I meet clients.'

Selling is helping a client understand the issues as well as providing a solution. All clients imagine that they know what they need, but in reality they are experts at what they want only, because they do not know the full range of solutions that exists.

They will say things like 'Not that there's much I can do about this...' because, like patients with the doctor, they are unaware of a treatment.

SHOW YOUR SOLUTION'S ABILITY TO PERFORM UNDER EXCEPTIONAL CIRCUMSTANCES

All organizations face occasional disasters, natural or otherwise. Finding out directly the sources of the anxiety can be helpful in two ways:

• It shows your company is keen to understand what might happen.
• It shows your company thinks ahead.

Often, the best way to do this is bringing together people from both sides for a meeting. The agenda might go like this:

1. What is the worst experience you have ever had with [e.g. storage systems]?
2. How was this dealt with?
3. If we change [the system], what would be your biggest worry? (Categorize the worries: technical, human, environmental and so on.) Has anybody ever actually experienced such a thing?
4. Who would be responsible for sorting this, if it occurred? (Sometimes responsibility is more worrying than the event.)
5. How far can these events be anticipated?

This is starting to produce a risk register before the solution has been agreed, but you are doing it to demonstrate that service is fundamental to your sales process and not something that only happens during delivery. Do not use this meeting as a chance to sell the fail-safe features built into your solution, as you may be tempted to do. This meeting is to consult and establish with the sponsor the degree of (in)security that is acceptable with the solution you propose. It also helps your specialists to understand the client's issues first hand.

Putting it all together

Your performance during the sales cycle informs the client what to expect in terms of service. This requires involvement of more than just you and the client – other stakeholders in both organizations will also need to take part. A positive experience gives both sets of 'clients' a good feeling about how risks will be managed proactively in the future.

45 SOLUTIONS SELLING IS A TEAM SPORT

'Consultants hunt in packs.'

Anon.

Selling solutions gets complicated quite quickly so, although the salesperson's responsibility is for opening up the lead and steering the process, this won't work in the longer term. People often describe selling as a lone-wolf sport or a numbers game: call enough potential customers often enough and in the end you will achieve your target. It worked for encyclopedia salespeople going door to door, so it will work for you. However, this is probably no longer the case if you are selling a solution more complicated than a set of fat books.

GET OTHERS INVOLVED BY SELLING THEM THE BENEFITS

A study of the most important attributes for client loyalty highlighted the following as being the 'top five' actions for sales reps who want to ensure loyalty. The client needs to know that you will:

- offer unique and valuable perspectives on the market
- help them navigate alternatives
- provide ongoing advice or consultation
- help them avoid potential landmines
- educate them on new issues and outcomes.

None of these attributes is surprising – they are all taken straight out of the playbook of trusted advisers – but they all have a considerable impact on the amount of time you can spend with customers if you are doing all the thinking work as well.

Salespeople are expected to have their own expertise about markets and competitors' solutions. This isn't a one-off expectation: customers want their salespeople to keep on broadly 'educating' them, showing them new ideas and tools and introducing them to risks they should be thinking about. When IBM moved from selling products to professional services in the 1990s, I worked with a group of educators from a range of professional firms running courses for salespeople to assist them in making the transition. We would ask salespeople, 'What knowledge or expertise do you have for which the client would pay you an hourly rate?' Salespeople mostly failed to answer because in the product world their expertise was about the product, not the client's business or the client's customers.

Most salespeople feel that the level of support they get is inadequate, whether this be researchers and analysts, market specialists, consultants or technical people. Sometimes these people are in a pool, juggling the demands of different sales reps. On larger bids, they tend to be assigned, but only when the prospect is looking hopeful. If these people are good, they will be in hot demand from every salesperson. You will have to persuade them that your case is interesting, has a reasonable chance of success and will help them to progress their career. To get support, you have to sell in-house.

The main benefits you can offer are exposure to clients, access to different work (when the project is won), skills in business development and being part of an ad hoc project called the campaign. They might even learn to project manage.

REWARD THE TEAM FOR PROGRESS AS WELL AS ACHIEVEMENT

If solutions selling is a group challenge, it requires leadership – thought leadership as well as motivational team leadership. Great salespeople think of each campaign as a project with themselves at the helm. They don't imagine they have to do all the thinking, but they define and challenge the parameters for that thinking. They don't regard the mix of skills and experience around the table in hierarchical terms, or indeed themselves as the customer and the analysts and specialists as the suppliers. They think of the project as a test of their collective professionalism, where everybody has a contribution to make and where every step to success will be celebrated. B2B selling should showcase the best of your business in front of your client.

Don't try to master everything yourself, but do try to choose the people who can both do the technical work and communicate this well to clients. The selection criteria are not that different from the 'good client' criteria already referred to. These people must be dedicated, sharp, demanding of themselves, self-starters who like to compete and win, and possibly insecure high achievers.

To save your energy, manage the campaign by deliverable and deadline: 'Four slides on what is happening in the oil and gas market in terms of prices, end-users, regulation and government involvement and then three slides we can use to stimulate the discussion with the director of drilling operations by end of the week.' If the team or the individual does a great job on this brief, consider bringing them to the meeting; they will do an even better job next time when they see how their work is used and this represents real recognition for the work they do. With time, they may be able to answer questions of detail, based on their research and analysis. This is also good for you; if you want to sustain your energy for the longer term, you will need others to step up in this way.

HELP THEM COPE WITH DISAPPOINTMENT

When junior professionals say dismally, 'I've just been doing business development for the last month', it means that they haven't been well led. No team always wins and the real test of your ability to motivate will be how you react to them when you fail. Post-mortem reviews are probably standard in most sales organizations, but doing them in a way that energizes the team that has lost takes skill. When you have shared any client feedback, 80 per cent will say that you lost on price, not because it is true but because it is easier to explain than 'You didn't make the case for value' (or 'We didn't trust you as much as the others' – even harder). Find out from the team the answers to these questions:

1. What would they do differently next time?
2. What did we do right that we should emphasize more next time?
3. What did we learn to carry forward into the next campaign?
4. What contributions stand out in terms of how individuals performed?

And then take everybody for a drink.

Putting it all together

You can't do it all on your own – sustainably. Building your team of support takes energy and commitment and this can be forgotten in the dash to the market. Those analysts and specialists are not waiting for your call. You need to bring them on board with your own professionalism about selling and leadership.

46 EVEN VILLAINS CAN BE GENTLEMEN

'A gentleman is somebody who is never rude unintentionally.'
Anon.

The ability to be polite, even when facing off to some pretty terrible people, is a useful quality for a salesperson. Being polite means that we are calm, diplomatic, able to ask interested questions and smile. Nature's aristocrats do this naturally, without thinking about it; whatever their background, they seem to be able to put just about anybody at their ease. They also seem to be able to influence others to do things that are often a bit surprising: lend them money, introduce them to the Duke of Westminster, buy them a beer.

The salesperson who suggested this secret was a true gentleman. He had been to a good school and wore a tailored suit. His shoes were of particularly good quality. He was solicitous about the welfare of others in any room he entered. You might have disliked him on first meeting him, but his relentless affability made this emotion almost impossible to maintain. You were simply charmed into submission:

'I'm often at a disadvantage in selling because I don't really look hungry enough. Apparently, if you don't really want it, the customers are going to be worried that they won't get such a good deal. You have to be "hot to trot", as the saying goes, which I, transparently, am not. But I have found that, if you treat people like decent human beings, this goes some way to getting them on side. I do a lot of nodding when I'm listening, like a rather demented toy dog in the back window of a car. I do find most of what people tell me quite interesting, but perhaps over-egg it a bit with murmurs of "Fascinating" and "Goodness!"'

The impact of this is to make the other people feel like gentlemen, too. If they feel like this, there is a fair chance they might start to act in the same way and their villainy will stay hidden.

VALUE RESPECT MORE THAN LIKING

Not everybody is trustworthy. Well-intentioned people may give you dire warnings about both organizations and individuals. Large corporations with escalating shareholder expectations can sometimes be the worst at dealing fairly with a vendor, yet their success cannot be entirely due to sharp practice. Often, their behaviour depends on the size of the deal; all client organizations have levels of scrutiny related to size of purchase order, just as sales organizations do.

One salesperson told me that he sometimes asks to take out references on a new client's company when and if the client asks him for the names of customers they could talk to. This takes some nerve, but does highlight that the solutions world really requires a relationship of equals. Mutual referencing may become more commonplace as sites like Uber expect both driver and passenger to be rated. In fact, there is no reason why, as seller, you shouldn't check out your client, especially if their Ts & Cs appear too draconian. If they won't pay 20 per cent up front, what does it suggest? If they won't honour 30-day payment terms, do you want to do business with them? When, as sellers, we give way to terms or behaviour that are unreasonable (by our standards), then agreeing to do business may not be so sensible after all, unless we check out their record with other suppliers.

Still, some clients will undoubtedly be villains and turncoats by their very nature, and when we discover this, we need to be careful about stereotyping them as such. Negative labelling prevents us from developing a relationship of trust with people, and is the root of prejudice and -isms of many sorts. Understanding what drives their villainy – not because we can 'fix' it – helps to keep us engaged. More experienced salespeople told me that they actually quite enjoy the challenge of difficult clients, of finding a way to overcome negative aspects of their behaviour that were being influenced by the environment – the swearing, the lateness to every meeting, the inability to make a decision. But they also accepted that, in the end, you just have to take some clients off your Christmas card list...

FIND SOMETHING ABOUT THE CLIENT TO ENGAGE YOU

If you can't like them, you need to find something that will engage you. Often, this is about setting a relationship management goal for yourself as well as goals that relate to progressing sales. This could be something as simple as 'I'm going to get her to smile in the next meeting'. Most clients have mannerisms, like most salespeople, and observing these and trying to understand their origin or inspiration will also help you to engage with the person, even if you can't stand them. See what happens when *you* behave differently.

When things go wrong and the client starts to take it out on you or your team, if the relationship is not positive, the tendency is to run for the hills. This is not the answer. A lot of difficult people behave in provocative ways to test suppliers and salespeople – your patience, your loyalty, your commitment. Pass the test and you move into a different league. If the client you are finding difficult has – surprisingly? – some loyal supporters around them, this test is often the reason for their unreasonable behaviour. If they have a new assistant every month, it is probably what they are like.

Many people under stress find it hard to disagree without becoming disagreeable. Their comments turn personal and the discussion heads for conflagration. Great salespeople seem to remain both calm and connected in these circumstances, able to think logically and behave tactically, even when under fire.

'You have to be something of a psychologist if you are dealing with senior people with large egos working under huge pressure. They need to look good all the time, and when things go wrong they know they will be criticized, so they strike out first, attack being the best form of defence. The main thing is not to make them feel that there is anything wrong in what they are saying or doing. It's natural. Expected. Normal. Dear respected client, you would be

inhuman if you didn't... scream obscenities, or whatever.
I find that sometimes when it blows over they apologize,
but not always. Admitting to a mistake – commercial,
managerial, personal – that's just too risky for them. So we
have to suck it up and carry on. But I find it interesting all the
same. You can learn to prevent these blow-ups with almost
everybody in the end.'

This is unless you are also a 'huge ego working under pressure...'

DRESS FOR RESPECT RATHER THAN TO IMPRESS

Dressing to impress is not the same as dressing for respect.
Polished shoes say respect but a bespoke suit or a large diamond
ring is possibly showing off. Gentlemen – and ladies, come to
that – want to put others at their ease, not compete with them in
the wardrobe department.

The rule, according to most men in sales, is be 'one level more
formal than your client'. This shows you have made an effort on
their behalf. If they wear a T-shirt and cut-offs, you wear a polo
shirt and jeans. If they wear a suit and tie, you wear cufflinks. The
key is to look professional, which for most men means following
'rules' about formality when there is some doubt about what
to wear. As you get to know your client and their organization
better, some of the rules relax and you can start to blend in, even
adopting their dress code in some situations. Imitation is the
sincerest form of flattery (as long as it is accurate imitation and
not parody). The days of the salesman's 'uniform' are gone except
for some commodity suppliers. Dressing 'like a salesman' might
be depressing the perceived value of what you sell.

The rules for saleswomen's dress are more complex. It's about
balancing looking attractive (which is subjective and differs
according on the gender of the person making the judgement)
with looking professional (a more subjective assessment for
women than men). The idea of being respectful of your client
still works as a guide: what would they find not just acceptable
but indicative that you had made a bit of effort on their behalf?
'I look at the website and see the models they use,' said one

saleswoman. 'It's never what they are really like, but can give you some insight into their ideal...'

Here is some research from the US:

- Women tend to like black: 51 per cent of female execs wear black compared with 26 per cent of men.
- Men tend to prefer blue: 36 per cent of male execs wear blue.
- Only 14 per cent of senior execs wear suits; 63 per cent now wear business casual.

For both sexes, the tension is between being authentically yourself and showing that you have made an effort. As one salesman put it:

'I don't ever wear a tie. I only own an old tie of my dad's, for funerals – but in media companies nobody does either, so that isn't a problem. The clients wear white shirts and dark suits, sometimes just the jacket and designer jeans, so I have a few of these in my wardrobe, but I tend to wear the whole suit, not the jeans. And I observe the "button rule": one undone during the day, two after six...'

Make of that what you will.

Putting it all together

As salespeople, we expect to meet some unpleasant clients from time to time. Their unpleasantness may be an aspect of their personality but it is more likely to be a function of their situation – or their *interpretation* of their situation. Anger is often a form of defence, for example; if you feel threatened, you erupt.

Dealing with the villains requires firmness about what you will accept and respect for them as people. Staying engaged in the relationship is key; if you withdraw or stereotype them, the game is lost. Paradoxically, those who behave worst often need what you have to sell the most.

47 PROXIMITY TO THE CLIENT PAYS OFF

'How did I "discover" gravity? By thinking on it constantly.'
Isaac Newton

If you have a big client account with many needs, you should be there more than in your own building. Great salespeople are often not that great at being available to their colleagues. Some are almost elusive. Great salespeople walk the client floors so that they become a familiar face to the organization and so that their presence is nothing unusual; this provides access and influence. Great salespeople are also account managers.

This goal may take many years to achieve and is possibly only worth doing for clients who can help you achieve your target as an individual account, but it has great merit, as this story indicates:

'I met Don in the bus going into Houston one evening on my way to the hotel from the airport. Don was second in charge of operations at the time and I had met him on a training course we had run with his company. He looked pretty shattered and wasn't the easiest person – a rather dour retired Calvinist minister who had migrated to software management – but I decided to recognize him. He gave me a rather watery look, as if to say "I'd rather not be interrupted" but I persevered and in the end he talked about the possible promotion to Operations Director that he was facing. Without thinking too much about this, I offered to help him plan his interview strategy, if he was willing – a free coaching session the following afternoon. It was a bit cheeky, I suppose, and he didn't look exactly thrilled, so I said I would drop by his office and he could decide.

'To cut the story short, the tactics we discussed seemed to do the trick and he became Operations Director. He then hired us to help him build his team and I worked closely with him to do this. During the offsite I had to coach him again to stop being too pushy and let others contribute more, which as a rather forceful person he found difficult and walked away in a bit of grump. Later, in the lift, we met a colleague in charge of services selling with whom he had a terrible relationship and I advised him to work on this as well. Again, he looked furious at being counselled in this way, and I thought I had lost the relationship I was building. In both cases, however, he did what I suggested and with positive results.

'I have worked with him off and on as a client now for over seven years; he isn't easy but I seem to have his ear when there are problems. That's all you can ask for as a person selling advisory services.'

Only by being there early can you benefit from what is happening at the later stages.

LOCATE YOUR OFFICE IN THEIR BUILDING

Being present is a huge competitive advantage. I once did a project with a professional services firm to help them to generate more sales. The project started with analysing where their largest and more profitable projects had had their genesis; in every case the answer was 'We were already in a dialogue with this customer when the opportunity arose' or 'We were already working for them when...' There is no substitute for being there when the crisis occurs or the need arises.

You should aim to have an internal phone extension that appears in the client company phone book. This has always seemed preferable to some rather meaningless label such as 'preferred supplier', which is mostly useful for consoling your manager that you have an inside track with this customer. If you can persuade your client that you can do more good by being there a couple of days a week, then you are halfway to doing this. From your client's point of view, they now have somebody to complain to and refer others to when and if things go wrong. But from your point of view you will have access to people and intelligence, which would require months of cold calls and staff meetings.

It is one of the great mysteries in the recognition of selling that repeat sales do not attract more credit than landing new customers. If you are part of the fabric of the client's site, then you will sell more and you will be able to tell your product and solution development people exactly what needs your customer has. Embedded account managers are moles, reporting back to their company on trends and concerns and plans.

BUT DON'T 'GO NATIVE'

This apparently racist notion probably has its origins in the experience of colonial administrators of the British Empire in the nineteenth century. Posted to some distant outpost with a plentiful supply of gin but not much else by way of support, they found themselves relating to the population they were supposed to be policing, organizing or supervising, to the extent that – shock, horror – they began to empathize with their oppressed state. Perhaps they even married a local and gave up the sola topi to wear more comfortable clothes.

Anybody who has been a project manager for any length of time will know you can't manage what you can't see. So most project managers have an office at the site, preferably near to their sponsor's. It works as long as they keep reminding their sponsor that they actually work for Company X and not his company. This is simply achieved by ensuring that the project manager attends training programmes and their own meetings at their own offices at regular intervals or on prescribed days of the week. The client cannot then take their presence for granted.

A management consultant expressed it like this:

'Of course, it is great to know that what you do is valued and that they want to retain our services, because we are helping them grow their business. But it isn't that big a step for the client to start to take you for granted and you find yourself putting together a PowerPoint for Monday's meeting, based on a briefing over the phone at 6 p.m. on Friday. It's sometimes hard to tell them you aren't their "slide bitch".'

LOCATE YOUR MIND IN THEIR OFFICE

'The test of all this is your ability to anticipate what clients might think or need next. You only start to become a mind reader when your mind is engaged in thinking about improving their business first and your business second.'

The more familiar you become with your client's business and the relationships between people in the organization, the easier it becomes to sell. People in different industries have variously tried to assess the different opportunity cost of sales between the first and subsequent contracts, but in general a saving of at least 30 per cent seems likely. Opportunities for services and solutions are everywhere in client accounts, but being surrounded by them every day does not mean that you will immediately spot them.

You need to think about this as your potential client(s) would. What is not working? What is the impact of that? Why is this not working? What can we do about it? By thinking about the client's situation on a daily basis and interacting with the clients themselves, you have a far better chance of getting something half right, as long as you do think proactively about what the client could do to improve.

Doing this thinking at the end of a contract prior to renewal is the wrong time. Clients are expecting upselling suggestions for new projects when the current contract runs out, so they have their objections prepared. They may be less ready to put you off if they receive your suggestions as part of an ongoing dialogue about building their business. Good professional services firms always think about the 'next project' as soon as they have closed the first one. But their ability to sell this will depend on their ability to understand their client's unique situation – which is harder to do in isolation from that business and much easier in the staff kitchen.

Putting it all together

When you are preparing to sell, you must think long term. Many companies do not organize their sales force around this idea; in fact, they do the opposite, which creates pressure on the salesperson to promote what may not be valuable for the client, except as a short-term quick fix.

For higher-value solutions this misses the main opportunity, which lies in the lifetime value of that client to your business. Until you think in a similar time frame to your senior clients – strategic, medium to longer term – you will be missing this opportunity and wondering why other competitors – consulting firms, for example – seem to have stolen the high ground from your company. Thinking in the longer term only really happens when you have an intimate knowledge of how your client's business functions on the basis of regular access to the issues, hence the need to aim to be located at their building, not yours.

48 STORIES INSPIRE AND REASSURE

'The story is an axe to the frozen sea within us.'
Franz Kafka

Storytelling is part of the salesperson's toolkit – the anecdote that illustrates the point, the well-chosen disaster recovery story, the parable or the joke. Stories help us present benefits in a subtle way. Stories lighten up the duller parts of pitches and meetings, because storytelling is social and, ever since we sat around the fire together, they have been part of our culture as human beings. Like trade, they bring us together.

Storytellers are often valued as entertainers in their own right and great salespeople love to tell stories. When I was interviewing people for this book, a question they were always delighted to answer was the story of 'the worst sales experience you ever survived'. Some of their tales have found their way into these pages, but because of the way the question was framed the heroes are the salespeople themselves. Stories appeal to the ego of the salesperson; it is a change to be the centre of attention, and great salespeople are aware that this is a mixed blessing.

'The first challenge is always to get the client's attention. You can't find out about their interests, needs or problems until you have engaged them. Stories engage people because they aren't just about what happened; the way they are told reveals something about you, the teller. So they connect you with the audience. There has to be conflict or drama in a story. That means emotion. The guy who cracks jokes is humorous. The guy who tells fables likes to teach. We learn about the storyteller from the experience of listening. That's why I tell stories. They introduce me. And if the client tells me a story in exchange, that's even better.'

MAKE THE CLIENT THE HERO OF YOUR STORIES

Several salespeople recommended this idea because it overcomes the tendency of the storyteller to sound big-headed. If you are praising your client – as Shakespeare's Mark Antony knew well – you sound as if it isn't about you, even if it is.

This is particularly important when discussing the benefits of your solutions or your company's track record of success. Never say, 'We delivered 30 per cent improvement in assembly-line productivity for Company X.' Always say, 'Company X achieved 30 per cent improvement in assembly-line productivity by using our solution.' Better still (if talking with a production manager), say, 'The Production department in Company X achieved 30 per cent improvement...'

It also helps, when making a pitch, to focus on what the client will achieve as a result of the purchase, rather than just what you will deliver. This is a fine balance to get right, because they are looking at what your company will deliver in terms of value for money, technical specification and whatever other criteria they have decided upon to compare offers. But emphasizing their situation, their objectives, their issues and even their contribution to the approach and their actions – it will start with their decision, after all – helps to make them feel ownership.

One of the reasons clients respond to stories is that, by hearing about other examples, they are enlightened about their own situation. As they listen – just we do when reading novels – they are implicitly comparing what they are hearing with their own situation. If the story is optimistic in outcome, they feel more optimistic. If the client concerned overcomes obstacles with your support, they feel inspired. There are few more subtle ways to excite a client's ambition, and storytelling can create the appetite you need.

EMPHASIZE THE LEARNING FROM
PAST MISTAKES

Another way to tell stories without sounding as if you are grandstanding is to tell cautionary tales about things that went wrong.

First, in the story, you take responsibility for what went wrong: 'We didn't manage the client actively enough', or 'We kept focusing on the medium-term target we had agreed and didn't consider…' This shows that you take your accountability seriously when you are hired and that you are prepared to put your hand up and be counted.

Secondly, you emphasize the positive outcome from the failure in terms of the client:

'It was going horribly pear-shaped at this point and the IT Director didn't have much hair left, but – hindsight's a great science – in the end, we probably needed that bad patch to really get the team together. It helped to deliver a fantastic result – 15 per cent more than we had promised, and we generally underestimate a bit, as you would expect…'

You might also emphasize that the client was material to the positive outcome:

'The IT Director was absolutely brilliant. He stuck with it and with us and, although these things aren't easy, he never lost faith in the project.'

Thirdly, you highlight the insight or learning from the experience, preferably for both the client and your company, but mainly for the client:

'We were too ambitious: one bite of the elephant at a time, and all that. We all agreed afterwards we had tried to eat the whole herd. The IT department never commissioned a project like this again, and we wouldn't take one on if a client asked us. It worked. It delivered, but it was too close. When projects stretch out over more than 18 months you know that needs change, sponsorship changes… there are horizons you can't predict. We encourage clients to be more modest and we are more flexible as a result.'

BE CONCISE; BE WITTY; ENTERTAIN

Comedians always say 'Leave the audience wanting more' and this is true of all storytellers. But being concise takes rehearsal and a bit of road testing – the first outing of a stand-up is never at the bigger venue. This means the salesperson needs to work on their act – to get feedback.

Here's a story that illustrates what rehearsal can do. It's not a sales story but it is about persuasion and using a story to influence thinking:

'We were doing a consulting project with a part of a government ministry to introduce a commercial cost-accounting system and had done the analysis. One of the things we had investigated was the use of the current cost code structure; each project was assigned a cost code and people were supposed to attribute all expenses, such as purchase orders, to that designated cost code. It's the basis for reliable analysis of costs, of course.

'A junior consultant had cross-checked about 100 purchase orders and found that there was an error rate of 18 per cent, but we weren't sure whether this was normal in government or not and so didn't know what the figure really meant; was the cost code system "useless" or just "failing a bit"? One of the budget holders interviewed had admitted to writing down car number plates on purchase orders when stuck for a cost code, so we decided that this story might be more persuasive than a figure, even with the accounts committee.'

They rehearsed the story with the consultant, who was a good storyteller anyway. His first attempt went something like this:

> 'I'm interviewing a budget holder and I pass him a purchase order form and ask him, "What do you do when you are uncertain about the correct cost code for the purchase order?" There's a bit of a pause and then he says, "I write down the first car number plate I can see out of the window."'

This was OK but not very persuasive, so they added a bit of emotional detail. The second version went like this:

> 'I'm interviewing a budget holder and feeling a bit uncertain about asking so bluntly about purchase order attribution. I don't want him to think I'm accusing him or anything. So I pass him a purchase order form and ask him, "What do you do when you are uncertain about the correct cost code for the purchase order?" There's a pause and he looks a little sheepish, but then he says – and these are his words, "Well, I look out of that window and I write down the first car number plate I see."'

They added a few gestures to the performance and the consultant told the accounts committee the sorry tale. They winced. The 'truth' of the story – which they probably already suspected – carried more weight than a bald 18 per cent.

Practice and rehearsals also fine-tune the language of the story to make phrases memorable. A well-phrased story is also easier to tell, as anybody who likes jokes will agree; dialogue and description (as in the example above) create opportunities for the storyteller to engage their audience, as do rhetorical questions. In fact, all the verbal tricks the ancient Greek orators deployed are worth borrowing for stories that you plan to use a lot: alliteration, paradox, puns and the rest.

An audience of other salespeople may not always be the best way to do this fine-tuning, as they may not always be representative of your client's style or culture. It may be better to ask a journalist, a speechwriter or a child; they give the best feedback.

Putting it all together

Stories make points that PowerPoint slides cannot. They engage people in what you are saying because there is an emotional element, often missing from unadorned argument. Using stories to educate and inform is nothing new and has the added advantage of making what you say memorable.

But it takes practice and rehearsal. In this way, your story and your telling of it improves. Your confidence enhances the experience, and if the client is central to the content it will not appear like an ego trip either. The best sales stories show what can be accomplished and help the client to understand that, with the right support, their outcomes can be achieved.

49 PROFESSIONALISM MATTERS, NOT JUST RESULTS

'Professionalism demands an unconditional regard for your client's problem.'

Carl Roger

Being professional means being in possession of a whole range of skills and techniques. This is a secret to learn as soon as you start your sales career, because many people begin by thinking that selling is about results more than professionalism. It is both.

> 'When I started out I wasn't sure I wanted to do selling. I thought I would give it a try and I was pretty hopeless for quite a long time. I had a good mentor who encouraged me and showed me that good judgement and confidence – both qualities in professionals – are learned by getting it wrong. But not repeating the same mistake.'

REVIEW WITH MORE EXPERIENCED PEOPLE

Professionals are valued for their good judgement, but this doesn't happen overnight. Discussing sales tactics and doing post-mortems with people who have more experience are the best ways to accelerate this process for yourself. In organizations this will ideally mean working either with your boss or with more experienced colleagues who want to help you.

Important aspects of professionalism – behaviour with clients, values of dedication to the task, to name but two – are generally only learned with feedback. Good feedback is precise and based on observation of behaviour, so, if you are doing a call with another person, always make the most of the opportunity to get feedback on your behaviour and its impact. Decide what you want the other person to comment on and let them know in advance. Then review this immediately after the meeting.

DEVELOP YOUR OWN STYLE

All successful salespeople can articulate what works for them (as well as for clients). But your personal USP covers a huge range of possibilities, such as:

- good humour
- attention to detail
- the ability to concentrate for long periods of time
- affability
- the ability to write good proposals.

'I'm not exactly easy on the eye. But I find clients really interesting. Really. A lot of my colleagues can be very charming, but I have learned to make my genuine interest a selling point. The clients know I want to find out about their business, about them, about it all. Genuinely. I don't quite know why I'm like this – I've always been curious and a bit shy. But I remember it was quite a shock to discover that I could turn this to my advantage.'

As impact is hard to assess, again you may need help to work out what works for you. Focusing on your strengths – especially the ones you don't recognize in yourself, but which others see – is a good place to start. Building on strengths may be more productive than trying to rectify what others see as your weaknesses.

ACCEPT THAT TO DO A GOOD JOB TAKES DEDICATION

Selling is hard work and requires a complex skill set. These skills are often not highly valued in the general population. As a result, people tend to describe skilful salespeople as having 'flair', 'charisma' and 'natural talent for selling', as if these were God-given attributes rather than the result of hard work.

You can be a lucky salesperson. It does happen. You work for a hot brand with a hot product that everybody wants, and all you have to do is negotiate and take the order. And the market is booming for what you sell. In these circumstances you don't need dedication; you just need to get the job and the sales are yours to lose.

But to be able to plan and reliably deliver sales of solutions is not like this. Fashionability and desirability play a far smaller part in client decisions. Consistent performance takes a concerted effort by you, the salesperson. You need to follow clients, track them, understand them and choose your moment. Hunting successfully when game is scarce is the test of the great hunter.

Putting it all together

Successful salespeople are committed to their craft. They work hard, not just for the rewards but also because they are professional about the work; they study, they seek feedback, they review their impact. Although each develops his or her own style, the common factor is the ability to communicate a confident judgement on a client's needs and issues. Professionalism takes time to develop, but all clients recognize it.

50 NOT ALL CLIENTS ARE WORTH INVESTING IN

'Internalize the Golden Rule of sales that says: All things being equal, people will do business with, and refer business to, those people they know, like and trust.'

Bob Burg

To sell B2B you will need to play a long game. The skills involved are different from those required for selling products and commodity services. One key change you will need to make to succeed is to shift from 'winning deals' to 'helping clients'. Helping is a different relationship from winning or, as one salesperson described it, 'helping your clients to win'.

Here's an example, told to me by a very successful career salesperson. We will call the two competing companies concerned Hewlett Packard (HP) and International Business Machines (IBM), but they could be any companies selling solutions. The HP salesperson tells it like this:

'HP and IBM were both in the final two for a large deal and I was fairly sure our bid had won, when I was called in to see the client. In his briefcase was the contract ready for signature. The conversation was going well when the client's phone rang and it was clearly IBM on the line. I thought, "How on earth do they know I am closing with the client?" In what followed I became even more incredulous...

'I heard the client say, "What? But that's impossible! How did you know *La Bohème* is our favourite opera anyway? And you have two tickets for this evening? That's unbelievable; my wife and I have been trying to get some for weeks... of course, of course, just let me check with her first... I'll get back to you. I'll get back to you straight away."

'The client hung up, made me his apologies and rang his wife. By this time I was silently fuming; all my plans were being undermined by a well-tailored bribe. It was galling but also impressive. Outflanked at the last hurdle.

'The client said to his wife, "You'll never believe this; IBM have just offered us the best seats for *La Bohème*. Tonight. I know. Incredible how (a) they knew and (b) they got the tickets. Are you free? Can you be? It would mean getting straight on the train in about half an hour as it starts at 7.30. Ah…" Suddenly the conversation cooled. "Ah… OK. No babysitter. Too short notice. Oh dear. Damn."

'I leaned forward. "You should go. See that show. The production has had amazing reviews. We'll babysit for you, if you like. I'll get my daughter to meet me at your house and we will stay with the kids this evening."

'The client looked amazed. He rang his wife. "Geoff – sitting in my office – has just offered to babysit. With his daughter." His wife agreed, and… we won the contract.'

The HP salesman is playing the long game: his aim is to win the war, not the battle. But he also wins the battle.

In the solutions world, where people stop making huge up-front payments and pay instead annual amounts for usage, licences and the like, the long term is crucial for the sales revenues. The days of hunting the mammoth and gorging on the carcass for a few days are over; everybody has moved on to farming and needs to learn to milk the cows.

Although everybody interviewed for this book would say that client lifetime value is what *really* matters, they would also say that their organizations rarely agreed – unless they worked for private partnerships that did not need to pay out regular and predictable dividends. Rewards and recognition are still focused on the individual who nets a new big fish against the competition, not the farmer who diligently produces smaller fish year on year. The myth of the hero salesperson is powerful and slow to change, even if the market is moving away from such ideas. In the same way, sales career structures tend to motivate people to move from smaller clients where the commission is less to larger-spending (larger corporate) clients. This does not allow for people to track high-flyers who move from one company to another.

CHOOSE CLIENTS WITH THE GREATEST FUTURE NEEDS

How do you recognize people with high – and continuing – needs? First, they are ambitious and superior to the majority of clients in every way. They tend to be more intelligent, more demanding, better-looking probably, and more capable of handling strategic and abstract arguments. They are also more mobile, competitive, and more dedicated and passionate about their work. To sum up, clients like this are hard work. The clients with the greatest needs are never the easy ones, even if they are personally charming when it suits them. They will give you a hard time, but – and this is the point – they will deliver and they will be loyal.

Good clients know the value of a reliable person who doesn't over-promise and who delivers what they say. This person will be a foil to their ambition. Over time, as the salesperson and the client get to know each other better, the salesperson can start to solve more complex problems for their client, crafting more tailored solutions, for example. This gives them an advantage over the company that has to pick up the RFP rather than crafting it. Then they move from being the supplier to becoming the business partner. This means they become privy to yet more information with which to anticipate things that their client might need, or even opportunities that the client might miss. With this sort of information and a bit more time, they might even earn the right to be trusted for the advice they give, if they play it correctly.

As decision-making gets more distributed and organizations get more distributed, picking good clients with high needs is also about influence. Who are the target company's high potentials? How do they behave? Whether formally labelled 'hiPo's' or not, these sorts of people often have more influence than their level of seniority might suggest. Make them your friend and you may score twice; they become advocates for your solution now, especially if it fits their change agenda as leaders; and they may over time let you advise them. Of course, faced with a company organization chart, such things are impossible to guess, but career progression data – from sources like LinkedIn – can often give you a guide to who the movers and shakers might really be in a senior group.

RECOGNIZE THE WIN–WIN IN LONGER-TERM RELATIONSHIPS

The cost of buying goes up almost as much as the cost of sales. If you lose your preferred supplier status – or the company doesn't consider such ideas worth while – then the buyer's cost of locating and choosing a new supplier has to be reckoned with. One of the classic texts on buying business services admits that 'price should not only reflect the given production conditions at the purchaser or seller but the entire functional relationship between the customer and the supplier'. Many industries – manufacturing is one example – rely on longer-term relationships with suppliers to develop their own business. Over time, the mutual understanding enables each to support the other. If this relationship is continuously broken, some of the potential benefits will be lost.

Buyers are often advised to buy as far back in the supply chain as they can, to reduce the costs of intermediaries. In fact, there are often reasons for those intermediaries' existence – they add value to the solution in some way. Remove them and the buying organization often discovers additional costs in terms of storage or communication. But working more closely with such suppliers can often provide benefits for both, as the Japanese automotive industry demonstrates. When your suppliers' own factories are located close to yours, the whole thing becomes cheaper and easier to manage. And the potential for advice from the supplier also increases as they see how the buying company extracts value (or not) from the partnership. This will not happen if B2B clients are not open to advice and a progressive view of the working relationship.

In terms of choosing clients, this indicates that you should also investigate how a new client you might be thinking of approaching relates to existing suppliers. Are they loyal? Do they stick with suppliers? Do they buy advisory and other services from the same suppliers? Although a more promiscuous customer might create an initial opportunity, they might be less open to advice and longer-term relationships.

LET YOUR CLIENTS BECOME DEPENDENT ON YOU

In the tech sector, renewal rates for maintenance contracts range from 70 to 100 per cent, depending on the category. The longer your association with the client has lasted, the greater will be the value of the relationship component to both parties. Although this can mean inertia and complacency, it doesn't have to. Mutual knowledge can be used to hold you both to account:

- You know your client's preferences: what they like to do, what they don't like to do and would rather pay you to do. You know what motivates them – their areas of vulnerability and their strengths.
- The client is also more knowledgeable about *your* company's true capabilities and may start to cherry-pick the things they think you do best.

Share feedback with the client about how each of you creates value – or misses out.

If you know their business well, this is a huge advantage to most clients. If you and your delivery team already know what is going on for them commercially, culturally and politically, it makes everybody's life a lot easier. (Professional services firms are often accused of making the client pay for their 'learning curve', which may result in the client frequently changing providers.) With time, you may even get to know the client's business in some respects better than they do; you and your delivery team are engaging with different parts of the business and possibly have more relationships than your sponsoring client. You become the 'spies' of your sponsoring client, reporting back on the progress of the implementation for certain, but also on other issues you have observed. Handled properly, these data provide potential for further sales as well as building the relationship.

Continuity means consistency. Change in the hands of a known supplier can be less threatening and easier to present as a useful improvement on what has gone before. For example, if you propose to outsource a function where the company has already been working harmoniously for several years, there may be less opposition from the people who have been taken in-house as part of the deal.

Putting it all together

Chemistry cannot be engineered in the long term. Salespeople can charm and cajole clients into signing once, but the payment for solutions in future will require a continuity of relationship.

To make it work for you, the relationship must be authentic, and the client you choose must be open to advice and potentially comfortable with a degree of dependence on you – not to mention trusting you with their children...

This has always been the basis for successful trading relationships since commerce began.

INDEX